FOL 3

Training the Gaited Horse

From the Trail to the Rail

Gary Lane

authorHOUSE®

AuthorHouse™
1663 Liberty Drive, Suite 200
Bloomington, IN 47403
www.authorhouse.com
Phone: 1-800-839-8640

First published by AuthorHouse 1/26/2009

ISBN: 978-1-4389-4430-2 (sc)
ISBN: 978-1-4389-4431-9 (hc)

Printed in the United States of America
Bloomington, Indiana

This book is printed on acid-free paper.

Training the Gaited Horse From the Trail to the Rail

By Gary L. Lane

Copyright 2009 by Gary L. Lane

Published by
Gary L. Lane
194 Hereford Road
Brodhead, KY 40409

SAFETY NOTICE: This book describes training activities intended to be carried out in barns, pens, and open fields and forests with young, untrained, or partly trained horses. Specific safety measures are described for some activities, such as making sure ropes, lunge lines, and reins do not tangle the trainer's arms or legs, but none of the activities described should be undertaken without regard for safety of horse and rider or trainer. Please examine facilities for unstable mounting blocks, damaged walls, fences with sharp edges, unneeded loose tack and tools and other hazards. Correct any safety problems before starting any training.

First Printing, 2009

DEDICATION

This book is dedicated to my lovely wife RUTH and the Tennessee Walking Horse, MR. T's PRINCE, for their devoted support.

"Leadership is the art of influencing and directing your horse to obtain his willing obedience in the accomplishment of a task."

Captain *G. L. Lane*

From the Trail to the Rail

FOREWORD

Have you ridden the trail with a friend whose horse's head is jacked up as high as it can be carried? Have you also noticed that the longer the horse is ridden in this position the more out of control the ride becomes? It is obvious neither the horse nor the rider is enjoying themselves.

How many times have you attended a tack auction where a huge hunk of metal was being presented and sold as a gaited horse bit? Or maybe you bought a gaited horse and the previous owner handed you the horse's bridle with such a bit attached and announced, "This is a Walking Horse bit." These are just a few examples of poor training methods currently being used.

I'm not sure where all the misconceptions about how to train gaited horses evolved. I do know there is certainly a better way. There is proof of that better way in watching the transformation in horses that were started with almost brutal methods and the change that comes over them when they are given the opportunity to relax their bodies and minds and carry their heads in a normal position.

I'm confident you are going to learn the better way by reading and studying this book written by Gary Lane. Gary has broken down the training process into easy to understand steps, easy for you and your horse. The knowledge you gain can be applied to any horse and will help you become a leader and friend your horse will respect and willingly obey. Enjoy the journey because the sky will be the limit on what you can achieve.

Susie Chirpas

Table of Contents

Chapter One: Leadership With Horses...1

Chapter Two: Building a Foundation..5

Chapter Three: Developing a Training System.....................................9

Chapter Four: Starting the Gaited Horse..12

Chapter Five: Controlling the Hindquarters......................................17

Chapter Six: Sacking Out (Developing a Calm Mind).......................22

Chapter Seven: First Obstacle...28

Chapter Eight: Ground Driving...32

Chapter Nine: First Ride..37

Chapter Ten: Understanding Foundation Gaits, Pace and Trot..........41

Chapter Eleven: An Explanation of the Walk....................................46

Chapter Twelve: The Classical Training Scale....................................52

Chapter Thirteen: Seat, Legs, and Hands...56

Chapter Fourteen: Developing Contact..62

Chapter Fifteeen: Teaching the Flat Foot Walk.................................68

Chapter Sixteen: Developing the Gearbox in the Walk.......................78

Chapter Seventeen: The Horse's Top Line..87

Chapter Eighteen: Tennessee Walking Horses
    and the Running Walk...96

Chapter Nineteen: The Missouri Fox Trotter and the Fox Trot..........102

Chapter Twenty: The Rocky Mountain Horse...................................107

Chapter Twentyone: The Single foot Rack.......................................113

Chapter Twentytwo: Solving Pace Problems
    and Re–training on the Ground...117

Chapter Twentythree: Solving Pace Problems under Saddle..............125

Chapter Twentyfour: Solving Trot Problems
    and Re–training on the Ground...135

Chapter Twentyfive: Solving Trot Problems Under Saddle................139

Chapter Twentysix: The Canter...144

Chapter Twentyseven: Shoeing Considerations................................149

Chapter Twentyeight: Show Gait Considerations.............................153

Chapter Twentynine: Mr. T's Prince..159

ABOUT THIS BOOK

This book takes into consideration training for the trail and for the show horse using the old time training technique of flat-foot walking a horse into a finished gait. I include the Tennessee Walking Horse, Missouri Fox Trotting Horse, and Rocky Mountain Horse breeds in this book for their easy smooth gaits. "Why not just pick one breed for a book?" My response is, all three breeds mentioned do a flat walk. Each breed can be taught the flat walk using the same training principles. The flat-foot walk will always be the best gait for training the gaited horse. Riding the flat-foot walk slowly with the proper head elevation will have many positive effects on smoothing out your gaited horse. The flat-foot walk is the gait of choice for safety on the trail and for developing timing for show ring considerations.

All horses are individuals with a natural baseline of behavior. Training is a fresh puzzle you have to put together with each horse. This book covers groundwork and developing leadership-training plans that can and will work for you. Keep in mind all the ground work is necessary for obtaining a calm mind. I recommend you read this book cover to cover. Then apply what works for you and your training program. Never lose sight of the intent of your work.

Take seriously the old judging rule, "Form must never be sacrificed for speed." I like the old cliché, "Don't ride your horse outside his head shake." I have my own saying, "A calm mind is a terrible thing to waste with speed." Running walk, fox trot, and four-beat self-carriage gaits are terrible things to waste on speed. It's been my experience that when people have gaiting problems, speed will come to the forefront in some form or fashion. I don't want to criticize all speed. Some owners love speed-racking horses and have a lot of fun with those horses. However, speed racking is outside the scope of this book.

If you become confused just slow yourself and the horse into a free walk (dog walk) and ride slowly developing the flat walk and on to the finished gaits. If instructions in this book at times seem too technical, just remember the simple intent to slow the feet and believe in yourself. Go for a long slow trail ride and feel for your gait. Finding and setting the horse in gait is not difficult if you apply yourself and get to know your horse using good sound leadership principles.

The science of gait analysis is not confined to one person's theory. This is an on going science with good people in every discipline. Understanding independent footfall and how the horse uses weight transfer from foot to foot will give you a thoughtful look at gaits to assist you in training. You do not have to be the foremost authority on gait identification to learn to ride your horse slow and give him time to separate his feet in a good flat walk. A good flat walk is around four miles per hour.

Gaits of horses are like any other endeavor. The more you observe and gain experience (feel) the better you become. The challenge for you is to observe the horse's feet and how the feet move in relationship with the horse's body. Individual horses show different kinds of timed footfalls, head nod, and overstride. Some horses have show ring animation. Others do not. Some horses will shake their head more while others will stride more, some will pace, some will trot, some will mix and match their gaits, some will require shoes, and some will go great barefooted. Consider your horse's natural ability and train to a sound standard that matches that ability.

The best way to learn is to never quit, just keep riding and looking for answers from the horse and within yourself. Seek self-improvement with good clinicians, trainers, and good horses. Always take the high road with sound training principles that will embrace a calm mind. The gaited horse will come through for you if you meet the horse half way with love and understanding. I firmly believe gaited horses can reach a high standard for trail and show with proper classical training.

In my opinion, the Tennessee Walking Horse, Missouri Fox Trotter, and Rocky Mountain Horse are the most popular horses on the trail today. Each of these breeds has a similar history. All three were developed by hard working people who needed a light horse for farm and pleasure. Today's trends lean toward the show world to produce a crowd-pleasing horse with more pace. The pendulum is starting to swing back to a using type horse for the huge trail population. Sound horse breeders are recognizing a need for a horse with good sense that is easy to gait. If you will take your time and look you can find this type. It will save you countless hours in training a gaited horse. The popularity of all three breeds will continue to explode on the trail or rail. To say one breed is better than the other is nonsense. A particular breed of horse is a personal choice for the owner. Who are we to say which one is better? They are all great with good, smooth, flowing gaits. I would challenge everyone to ride a good Tennessee Walking Horse, Missouri Fox Trotter, and Rocky Mountain Horse.

No matter what your training goals are, trail riding or showing, I hope this book in some way helps you understand the gaits, training, and re-training for a great gaited horse that meets your needs. Enjoy the journey, be safe, and have fun.

Happy Trails,

Gary Lane

From the Trail to the Rail

ACKNOWLEDGEMENTS

There are many people I wish to thank for helping me write this book. All the students at clinics, trail rides, and horse shows whose friendships have taught me much more than I can ever repay them.

Pat Hooks a wonderful teacher and friend. Pat understands a better way to teach students and horses making the world a better place.

A special thanks to Alonzo Naiper and Dale Myler. Both men are good teachers who coach towards achievement with proper bitting.

Allanna Jackson and her mare *Sacia's Pride* who displayed the proper trail gait standard. Allanna spent many hours critiquing the gaits and listening to me with long phone conversations.

Wanda Burdine, Meloney Meritt, and Dr. Lynn for proof reading and giving of their time freely looking over the pages in this book.

Charlie Roach, a good clinician and dedicated farrier who strongly advocates shoeing for a balanced foot.

Jessica Lynn and her horse *Blue Kentucky Moon* with the photos showing the flat foot walk. A special thanks to Randy Mitchell for all his help at clinics and trail rides.

An appreciation goes to Roger Renner, a good friend and good horseman in his own right. Roger sets the perfect example for proper leadership in the community with a smile and a willingness to make other peoples' life better without pay. Acts of unselfishness are a characteristic trait of a true leader.

Anita Howe's work on judging standards for the modern day horse based on correct training philosophy. Observing Anita and her horse *Papa Royal Delight* is most certainly an opportunity to see poetry in motion. Seeing is believing.

A special thanks to Dyan Westvang and her knowledge of the old time Missouri Foxtrotter's smooth gaits in the Ozark Mountains. One has to appreciate the efforts of Dyan Westvang to keep the old bloodlines in the forefront with an ever-changing industry.

A thanks goes to David McGuire for his knowledge regarding the Rocky Mountain Horse and preserving the old bloodline for future generations to enjoy the traditional Rocky Mountain Horse.

Special thanks to Walter and Janet Stilwell and their horse, *Chance For Sun*, whose flowing gait was an inspiration to watch and observe in country pleasure classes in Kentucky. This horse won many blue ribbon championships and set the proper example for a correct sound Country Pleasure Horse.

A very special thanks to my Father Cliff Lane, Uncle Clyde Lane, Aunt Francis Mitchell, and Uncle Jim Lane. A creative family from rural Kentucky during the depression years lived in a tent beside the railroad tracks. This family set the standards for the spirit of achievement.

GLOSSARY

These specialized terms appear frequently in the book. If they are not familiar to you, please refer back to them as needed.

Arched back: The horse tends to carry a slight bow in its back. This can create a tendency to trot.

Art of Slow: Taking the time it takes to train a young colt on the ground and riding slowly.

Balance: When the rider is seated in balance with the motion of the horse. The sweet spot just behind the withers where the motion of the horse is like the balance point of a teeter-totter.

Calm Down Cue: Working the horse with the head below the withers for endorphin release.

Dog Walk: Ordinary four-beat walk on loose reins used to teach the flat walk.

Flat Walk: The flat walk is an even four-beat gait, energetic and bold with a sense of purpose. The horse should show rhythm, relaxation and looseness. The horse should nod his head with counterbalance of motion starting from the rear end with an overstriding step. The overstriding step should be the natural step with respect to the particular gaited horse breed.

Fox Trot: The fox trot is an uneven diagonal four-beat gait with head-shake and with legs that support on opposite corners because the horse breaks up the two-beat trot into a smooth ground-covering gait giving a unique rhythm and sound of a broken trot. An old foundation Fox Trotter hits a cap (sets the hind hoof on top of the front track) with little overstride.

Gait: One complete stride when all four legs have moved once.

Half Halt: Natural aids of pushing with the seat, squeezing with the legs, catching the energy with the hands, then releasing into gait.

Hollow Back: The horse is weak in the back with tendencies to carry a low back in the top line causing the horse to pace with a high head and hindquarters trailing out behind.

Hot Off the Leg or In Front of the Leg: When the rider squeezes with the leg the horse responds immediately by going foward with more driving action from the hindquarters, not speed. Keep speed out of it.

From the Trail to the Rail

Leadership: "The art of influencing and directing our horse to obtain his willing obedience in the accomplishment of a task." G. L. Lane, CAPT. U.S.A., Retired

Level Topline: Where most of the middle gaits can be found using the horse's back.

Middle gaits: The four-beat gaits found between the pace and trot: stepping pace, running walk, self-carriage walk, rack, and fox trot.

Natural Head Carriage: The height where the horse wants to carry his head naturally. With some horses the natural head carriage can be too high in the set period. See Set Period.

One Rein Stop: The rider uses one rein to disengage the hindquarters and releases the horse's face when the feet stop moving.

Overstride: The distances the hind foot over steps the track (print) of the front foot.

Pace: A two-beat gait with the horse using lateral pairs of legs working together on each side of his body. At the hard pace the feet lift off the ground on the same side in unison. Very rough to ride shifting side-to-side motion with suspension.

Rear-end Under and Front-end Across: Rolling the inside hind leg over the outside hind leg for disengagement then leading the horse's front-end back across to reverse the direction of travel.

Release Into Gait: When horse starts to flat walk release into gait for a reward.

Running Walk: Same foot fall pattern as the flat walk with more speed. Even in timing with headshake and overstride.

Self-carriage: A horse that can carry a rider using his hindquarters on a loose rein.

Self-carriage Gait: An even four-beat gait as seen with old foundation Rocky Mountain Horses found in Eastern Kentucky. Even in gait with over stride. Not a flying stepping pace or rack.

Self-seeking Reflex Action: The horse reaches down and forward for his own relief. The horse finds its best movement.

Set Period: The horse's learning time between two and four years of age.

Sequence: The order of footfall.

Stretching Into Contact: With outside rein contact the horse stretches down and forward. The rider feels the stretch as elasticity in the reins.

Square: A horse doing a good walk even in gait, with headshake and overstride.

Tension and Stiffness: Found in the top line, or back, with pacing and trotting horses.

Timing: The hoof beats in each stride.

Too Slick: A horse that exhibits too much pace.

Too Square: A horse that exhibits too much trot.

Top Line: For training purposes, the area of back muscle from withers to hindquarters.

Training Scale: Six steps in training to develop a horse into a trained or finished horse. The concepts of: (1) rhythm / relaxation, (2) looseness, (3) contact, (4) impulsion, (5) straightness, (6) collection.

Trot: A two-beat gait with the horse using diagonal legs in unison. Left front and right rear one beat. Right front and left rear one beat. Very rough bouncing motion up and down in the saddle.

Up Side Down Horse: A high-headed, hollow-backed horse with a stiff neck that has a dip right behind the withers that will slide the rider's seat into an unbalanced, feet on the dash board position.

Weight Support: How many hooves are on the ground supporting the horse's weight at specified points in the stride.

Chapter One: Leadership With Horses

"We cannot train without planning and we cannot teach without preparation." General George S. Marshal

In 22 years of training soldiers and horses I've begun to see very strong leadership correlations. Soldiers and horses both learn by doing hands-on training.

The mission of the Kentucky Military Academy is to commission young men and women as second lieutenants to lead soldiers in time of peace and war. Whether we want to admit it or not, freedom is paid for in the price of blood. I realized in the Gulf War that our nation's youth are our country's greatest national treasure.

One of the greatest opportunities of my life was to command the 223rd Military Police Company in the 1991 Gulf War. I remember the haunting looks of intense concern and focus of the family members as they hugged the troops prior to leaving. I was standing by the door just watching the troops when mother after mother approached me with tears in her eyes. Each would ask me to bring her son home safely. I had 190 of them to bring home safely. The 223rd Military Police Company played a vital role in guarding and transporting 22,000 enemy prisoners of war from Iraq to Saudi Arabia. I realized then, as now, I would continue to train with intensity and purpose, whether teaching young aspiring second lieutenants, young horses, or students at clinics.

The young officer candidate student is given the opportunity to make mistakes and then corrected until the student meets the performance standard for that task. The student is placed into every possible situation in leadership roles to prepare them for wartime missions.

Before I became the academy's senior instructor, I was an academy instructor. I learned that each lesson must be broken down into as many steps as possible to ensure meaningful training. If simple steps were left out it would jeopardize the achievement of the task standard later. If the lesson plan was nothing more than putting on a pair of socks I wanted the lesson broken down into as many steps as possible, i.e.: Sock size, sock color, wool or cotton, blister protection, how many socks to carry, and how often to change the socks. I think you're getting my meaning.

Four fine young captains were the academy instructors. They wrote lesson plans and submitted them for my review. Once the plans were approved the instructors conducted the training to standards. Working in the field with the soldiers was the most rewarding and gratifying time at the academy. Young soldiers retain training better when they see the big picture broken down into steps using hands-on training. No matter what the task, nothing can be insignificant and left to chance. Leaders are developed through hard work, discipline, and time.

The same is true with young horses.

With General Marshal's quote in mind, going to the barn to train a horse without a game plan makes for a long day. There is no sense shooting in the dark by not having a good training plan. A good training plan helps to develop a sound mind for your horse at all ages. I believe a good solid training plan is the key ingredient that separates good training from bad training. Effective training builds proficiency, teamwork, and confidence for you and the horse. I also cannot overemphasize having a safe plan with predictable results that minimizes inherently dangerous training risks. A safe and efficient training plan can be a simple plan or a complicated plan. You can make the call.

I use a simple plan that has worked well for me over the years. I call it tasks, conditions, and standards coupled with a safety program. Give this idea a try and see if it can assist you in developing your own training plan. There is nothing written in concrete that states you have to develop your plan exactly the same way I develop mine. Just get a feel and develop you own plan, breaking each area down into three concepts of tasks, conditions, and standards.

The task is what it is your want to teach the officer candidate, or the horse, for the day's lesson. You develop the task list, break it down into each piece or step involved in the task. You can train on one task or you can get complicated and multi-task. When starting the training of a young horse I highly recommend you train on one specific task at a time, breaking down the training into many small steps.

Conditions of the training take in two areas of concern: The equipment and the environment. You must have a working knowledge of the equipment and how to use the equipment safely and correctly. Conditions also take into account the weather and how it will impact your training. Teaching a young horse to lunge in the middle of field during a lightning storm is a daunting task. Know your weather forecast for today's training and adjust accordingly. Your local weather plays a big part in successful horse training. Military officer candidates learn to complete their tasks and keep their troops safe in all kinds of conditions.

Standards in horse training are not set in stone. Who sets the standards? Absolutely you! You, the owner, are responsible for the horse's training and welfare. However you want to measure the standard you've set is up to you. If you decide to use numerical percentage system, 10% through 100% is fine. A word system where you can use bad, not so bad, good, and finished would also be a good system.

You need a standard of training that recognizes improvement. When the horse gets better at the task, recognize the improvement, reward him and move him up a notch. A system to gauge and see improvement is very satisfactory within itself. The system also needs to recognize when the young horse's learning curve takes a step backwards. Adjust his score. Go back to what he can do well. Train to standard then move on towards the finished horse.

I place my own spin on defining leadership: "Leadership is the art of influencing and directing your horse to obtain his willing obedience in the accomplishment of a task." If you can influence and direct your horse, you can train your horse to a high level of performance in light shoes, but it takes time and patience. Knowing when to request more and knowing when to back off in training is a tough challenge even for seasoned veteran leaders.

Leaders are trainers, and trainers are leaders. The two words go together like hand and glove. All the horse wants is for you to be tactically and technically proficient in order to take care of his needs. A good tactical leader has prepared the horse for the field environment well in advance at home. Nothing is left to chance with the colt's training at home. He was developed to meet the challenge of trail or the rail. Then all the leader has to do is support the young horse and ensure his first few trail rides are a positive experience.

The horse has the ability to read you. Not only will he read you, he reflects your character in his behavior. The horse will also exploit your character flaws. A horse will always give us feedback about how the training is going. It amazes me how often the owner doesn't recognize the feedback. For example, when working trail obstacles at home, if the colt jumps across the obstacle instead of slowly walking across, he just told you he will jump across most logs on the trail. The horse's behavior shows if you know the right answers. There is nothing magical about his intuition. He is reflecting your training. If you don't have it right, don't blame him.

You can hear owners say, "I did not teach the horse that nasty habit. He picked it up from the previous owner." That may be true, but you, the current owner, are now responsible for the horse's behavior, what he does and doesn't do. As a good leader, you accept and take responsibility for his actions. Selling your horse because you can't get along with him and trying to get Mr. Right can be a long, tiring process. Certain owners make the same mistakes over and over again. They get the same problems with every horse they own.

Some owners always find something wrong with a leg or hock that conveniently keeps them from riding and training. Now it seems to me this is just an excuse to justify their fears of riding or the responsibility to train the horse. Most people who don't get along with horses don't recognize that the fault is probably within them.

Not every owner and horse combination is going to click with each other. If they don't there should be a parting of the ways. It is the owner's responsibility to ensure the horse goes to a good home with a new owner who is willing to spend the time in training the horse.

The responsibility of breeding and raising foals is much more demanding. You now have ethical and moral responsibility for good training and health care of the foals.

Sometimes there are trainers, or military leaders, who think they can slide through the training process without a hitch. Trust me on this one. The soldiers will go the extra mile for a leader they can trust. So will horses. Horses can separate a good trainer from a bad trainer with one eye closed. Some of those want-to-be horse trainers go on and start horse-trading barns with kid-broke horses in every stall. If you start asking the right questions the horse trader will brush you off quickly to the point of being rude. He does not know the answers, nor will he take the time to learn through study and hard work to develop the leadership skills necessary to start and train young horses.

Finding a role model in your community that you respect who will take the time to teach you leadership skills with a horse is priceless. Believe it or not, it does not have to be a human. More than one God-sent horse has taken the time to teach a human and explain the secrets of his kind in a simple way only a master can teach. Now I'm not saying you can't develop your relationship with your horse into a God-sent relationship. I believe you most certainly can, but most of us will need help from a good human role model. I've often wondered, who was the first human who rode the horse? Someone had to teach him. I wonder how he got the idea that a horse could become the greatest servant in the world? I do think there was divine intervention.

Understanding leadership and the role it plays in making you a better trainer is a good investment for you, the horse, and the situation. Knowing yourself and seeking self-improvement are keys to success.

The following chapters are time proven methods that have worked for me year after year. I use these methods first and foremost to teach a calm, trusting mind in the colt. I believe the classical training scale used by the great masters is the method that will stand the test of time. It can't be improved. A calm mind and a relaxed horse will develop into a proper trail gaited horse that is a joy to own and ride.

I like to watch a good clinician work a horse. Most have never been in the military, let alone a combat zone, but you can rest assured they are teaching leadership no matter what spin they put on the lesson. They say, "Hind sight is twenty–twenty." If I could go back in time to the Kentucky Military Academy and change one thing to make officer candidates better leaders, I would require each officer candidate to train a colt to improve his or her leadership traits. Take care of your own character to train your horse.

Chapter Two: Building A Foundation

Riding a horse is not a gentle hobby, to be picked up and laid down like a game of solitaire. It is a grand passion." Emerson

It all comes down to a calm mind. When things are going well, it's because your horse's mind is not bothered. If things aren't going well, a key point has been jumped, which invariably causes a problem with the horse.

Now it makes no difference if you're starting a young gaited colt or trying to improve your horse of many years. It all comes down to foundation training. A lot of people will tell you what good foundation training is, but only a few can tell you how to accomplish the training. There are many people who believe young two-year-old gaited horses are ready for the trails. They are not. It's been my experience you are just getting started with their education.

When a horse is evading or resisting his training, most of the time he is actually attempting to figure out what we want. More times than not, we see this as a direct challenge to our authority.

You find people who think older horses are wiser and safer, but without proper foundation training that older horse will just perfect every trick in the book to see if you really want to ride. The horse did not wake up one morning and say, "I'm going to develop every nasty trick in the book to make life miserable for my owner." The reason the horse develops every trick in the book is he had to go it alone. The foundation training was missed. The horse had no one to teach him how to behave, no one to support him or give him an opportunity to slowly develop his mind and body.

More and more horses are being culled at commercial training barns because the horse did not make with quick fixes and gimmicks. You will often hear trainers say, "He's not good enough for the show ring but would make a good trail horse." But without proper foundation training the horse won't be good enough to be a trail horse either.

Now these so called trainers may go through 100 colts to find five or six colts that have super athletic talent. Even with all the talent they find and keep most colts won't see the show ring at three.

I'm not picking on the gaited horse show horse industry. The other horse industries have just as much abuse of wasting good horseflesh at two and three years of age. For example, look at the horse racing industry. A colt that is trained outside his ability to understand at a young age will never make a good trail or rail horse. The point I'm trying to make is, give the colt a chance to reach his full potential without shotgun (mind blowing) training methods. I'm a firm believer that more horses would make great partners if only given the time to develop a good foundation.

The horse is made of pain, fear, muscle tone, and excitability. If all four areas are not balanced, gaping holes will appear in your training program. Training the horse as a whole using these four areas is essential for the overall mental health balance that will produce a calm horse.

There is much more to be done than just teaching the colt to ride. The colt has to be taught how to use his body and how to carry himself in balance. Now if you think training a colt to ride and training a colt to use his body in balance are the same thing you just fell off the cliff. There is big difference! Just plain riding your horse without regard to his mind and balance leads to a majority of the problems facing horse owners today. The colt that learns to carry a rider in balance is a more athletic animal with a calm and trusting mind.

One of the great mysteries that elude so many people today is getting the horse to walk off his rear end. If the horse doesn't have a calm and trusting mind it will never happen. Working to produce a horse that can walk off his hindquarters, whether on the trail or rail, is a goal for all horse owners. The pride you feel when your gaited horse shifts his balance to the rear and walks with low range overstriding power is the highest honor you can obtain in the equine world.

The more I train the trail-gaited horse, the more I am convinced that his heart and soul is in his mouth, and the gait is in his top line. The old-timers used to say, "The higher the horse's head, the less brains and the lower the horse's head, the more brains." Let's put a different spin on this and also say that, "The higher the horse's head, the less gait and the lower the horse's head, the more gait." The reason for this is when we raise the horse's head too high, his back is more likely to hollow and disconnect the horse's hindquarters from his mouth. The horse has to be ridden from the rear forward.

The flash and bang of the show world tends to create a high-headed horse that, unfortunately, carries over into the trail-gaited world. Now I don't want to discount the significance of the show world, for it has its place. But both worlds need to stretch the top line. What I mean by this is, if we can round the horse's back and ride the horse in a round shape, it can and will put our gaited horse in his natural shape. Then when we do raise the horse's head, it will cause the horse's withers and back to lift, thus lightening the forehand.

If the great masters of the twentieth century, or earlier, would have had the talented gaited horse of today, who knows what level of achievement could have been obtained? Most certainly, we would have a different equine world.

As I think of the great masters' training scale: (1) rhythm / relaxation, (2) looseness, (3) contact, (4) impulsion, (5) straightness, and (6) collection, I realize that you must have these six areas to train your horse successfully. They apply to all gaited horses. Using this training scale as tasks, conditions, and standards will develop and teach all equine owners a system that can maintain the welfare of the horse during his career and well beyond. This scale is so vitally important it must be committed to memory. The training scale gives you a starting point to develop your own system. The fascinating points about the training pyramid are time-tested results. When training is going good or bad it is the result of the application of the training scale using tasks, conditions and standards.

The bottom line is, it does not matter what gaited horse you ride, a Tennessee Walking Horse, a Missouri Fox Trotter, a Rocky Mountain Horse, or a Racking Horse it is the first three areas of the training scale where we get into trouble with our gaited horses. Why? It is because we ride outside his (1) Rhythm / Relaxation, (2) Looseness, and (3) Contact.

In order for us to be successful on the trails, we must identify two common problems with our gaited horses. The first is the horse's head is too high. The second, the horse is ridden too fast. Both problems can be solved using the training scale.

I believe our trail horses have to exhibit their foundation gait. You need some understanding of what this gait looks like and more importantly, what it feels like.

Because it is so important that you know how to identify the gaits of your horse I will discuss gait identification, achieving the gait, and understanding the gait in later chapters.

But before your horse can gait properly and consistently, the horse has to learn to relax. Don't be fooled, a great trail horse can do both areas, the trail or the rail, but the first step is to develop your horse's calm and trusting mind.

To have a great horse we have to show him the ground first (lower his head). I would like to share with you some sacking out exercises that will get you on the right track to develop your horse's mind. You must look at sacking out as much more than getting your horse used to scary objects.

The more ground work you do with the horse the safer and calmer the horse will become. A horse that has a good foundation in ground work (sacking out) will be a joy to own at five years of age. It always amazes me to watch what I call the "delayed training reaction" in horses. A colt that receives good sacking out training between the age of two and four (especially the difficult colt) will level out with a calm and trusting mind around the age of five years old. If you feel inside yourself and observe the colt closely you can feel the tension or calmness inside the colt.

The horse left without groundwork has no direction and guidance. He could still make a great horse and some do, but many more develop gaping holes in the training foundation. Look at it this way, sacking out training is a future investment for your safety. Giving the young colt an opportunity to learn to have a calm and trusting mind should be every owner's goal. The colt comes to us as prey animal. Nothing will change his wiring. When we teach with love and patience, getting the colt to accept the demands of the trail and show world, the results are unbelievable.

From the Trail to the Rail

Chapter Three: Developing a Training System

"Soldiers and horses both learn by doing hands-on training." Gary Lane

A colt coming out of the field I consider a green colt.

A colt that has been started for two or three months is a starter colt.

A colt under saddle that is learning to square up his gait and work off his hindquarters is a training level colt.

I lump this into one time period that I call the set period.

A horse that exhibits a calm, trusting mind, correct gaits, and works off the hindquarters with a light touch is a finished horse. The finished horse takes me on the average of two years of training in the set period (between two and four years of age).

I use a simple plan. I call it tasks, conditions, and standards coupled with a safety program. The task is what it is you want to teach the horse for the day's lesson, whether it be putting on a halter, leading, grooming, saddling, or whatever. You develop the task list, break it down into each piece or step involved in the task. You can train on one task or you can get complicated and multi-task. Starting a young horse I highly recommend you train on one specific task at a time. Break down the training into many small steps.

Now for what I mean by multi-tasking: For example, taking the horse to the cross ties, grooming him, tacking with the saddle, and bridle. You may think there is nothing remarkable or multi-tasking about leading the horse to the cross ties, grooming him, then putting on the saddle and bridle. Think about it this way. Just to lead the horse to the cross ties somebody had to catch the colt, gain his trust, teach him to be caught, teach him to wear the halter, teach him to give to pressure, teach him to respectfully follow the handler and teach him to stop, just so you can lead him to the cross ties. Standing tied in the cross ties is a new task.

The point I'm trying to make is this, for the sake of the horse's mind in the beginning of his training, teach one task at a time. Break each area of his training down into small steps building one step at a time to the next step. The more steps you can break the training into the more effective your training becomes. It is this concept that makes a master trainer truly a master trainer.

The number one problem area in training that causes more blown fuses with horses is training fifteen things at once. Some trainers at day one start riding a colt up and down the barn hallway. The majority of trainers don't realize they are overloading the colt's mind with signal after signal.

Now most certainly as the colt develops and gets consistent with his training he does and will accept very difficult multi-tasking as routine. It has to start out with just one lesson (task) at a time broken down into many small steps.

Conditions of the training take in two areas of concern: The equipment and the environment. Year after year new bits and saddles are added to the market. It's absolutely mind boggling which bit or saddles to use or not to use. With saddle makers you find very little common ground between companies except they all want to sell you a saddle. Going to large trade show in your area will give you some idea of what is going on with the horse industry. Most of the time you will find factory representatives who will answer questions.

It stands to reason that if you use equipment you're going to have to have a maintenance program. Somebody is going to have to clean and maintain the tack. More than likely it's going to be you.

The environment takes into account where you are conducting the training. Will you be working in a barn hallway, arena, or round pen? If your task list calls for lunging, starting in the middle of a forty-acre field with a green colt makes little sense because you're just setting yourself up to have problems. Working indoors or in a small enclosure makes good use of safe conditions for teaching the lunging lesson.

Conditions also take into account the weather and how it will impact your training. Your local weather plays a big part in successful training. Teaching the colt to lunge in the middle of field during a lightning storm is a daunting and dangerous task. Know your weather forecast for today's training and adjust accordingly.

Standards are not set in stone. I'll say this again: Who sets the standards? You! Standards give your horse an area of operation that is acceptable and what is not acceptable. I certainly believe there is a standard of conduct for your horse to attain and also a standard of performance on the trail or rail. If one day you let your horse nip at you and the next time you knock his head off it is unacceptable standards on your part.

Set the standards and enforce them consistently for the colt's behavior to achieve the desired results. There is no room for indecisive behavior on your part. Stay on the same playing field with same standards of conduct. Most horses, no matter the age, can learn to behave within the standards of conduct if you consistently enforce the standards. A horse truly wants to please his owner.

Most conduct problems are with your ability to handle the horse and set the standards. Medical problems can and will affect your horse's conduct. Don't be too quick to hand out undeserved harsh punishment. The standard of performance will change (sometimes daily) as the colt develops into his area of his expertise.

Where do you find role models to set your standards? Find a friend who has a finished gaited horse. Look at the qualities of that model horse. Ask yourself some questions. Does the horse have a calm and

From the Trail to the Rail

trusting mind? Is the horse safe to ride on the trail or the rail? Does the horse exhibit the proper gaits? Is the horse soft and balanced off the rear end when he walks? The list can go on and on as you become more aware. In my opinion, a finished horse is the standard we all strive to achieve with proper training and time.

We must not overlook the show ring. Now more than ever there are some great horses with eye catching, head shaking, flat walking ability. The right horse meets good standards both on the ground and in mounted work. Keeping the correct standards is your responsibility both on the ground and under saddle. Giving praise for every good effort your colt gives is good old common sense training.

I write all my lesson plans using task, conditions, and standards. I keep a training journal on each colt I train. When I sell the colt I give the training journal to the new owner. I recommend to the owners that they continue to use the journal and follow the colt through the same training outline. You will be amazed how this has helped owners establish a good relationship with their new horse.

The safety plan must be built into your training plan and be part of your training leadership style. Think ahead of the horse and determine what is going to happen before it happens.

✔ The safety plan should include you and your horse. Let's take it a step further and include bystanders. I require all my students to wear helmets during groundwork and riding.

✔ Keeping the horse calm before, during, and after a lesson is just plain good common sense. One of the lessons we want to achieve is a calm mind. When a horse is calmer after the lesson it is a strong indicator the lesson went well.

✔ Remind yourself to not let the rope get wrapped around your hands or feet. Keep your training area free of junk or other items that can get tangled in your feet or the horse's feet.

✔ I've seen more people hurt getting on a horse or getting off a horse. The one glaring fault was the rider did not have enough upper body strength to get on and off the horse and was not using a mounting block correctly. Your safety plan leaves nothing for chance and covers all areas of safety.

Taking the time to develop a training plan helps ensure success and will keep you working towards your training goals. Using tasks, conditions, and standards sets the tone for a lifetime of achievements. The idea I'm trying to get across is you don't have to start ten horses a year, one horse can be a lifetime of learning and teaching.

Chapter Four: Starting the Gaited Colt

"The greatest power is often simple pleasure." E. Joseph Cassman

One of the key things to remember when starting the young horse is no one ever ruins a young horse by training too slowly. I'm a firm believer that the slower you train the young horse the faster you go. The young horse starts his training with you like a clean sheet of paper. You fill in the blank lines one line at a time. You need to ask yourself some questions to determine if you are ready to undertake the task of starting a young horse from the ground to the trail.

(1) Do I have time to take on this commitment?

(2) Do I have the equipment and facilities to work the horse safely?

(3) Will I see this commitment through?

(4) Do I have support from a competent professional or friend?

(5) Have I observed this process from start to finish at a good training barn?

(6) Do I understand safety before, during, and after the training session?

The list of questions can go on and on. Hopefully you've answered "yes" to the questions and have a "can do" attitude. Now I don't have to hang my common sense on the barn door thinking that I can teach you all you need to know in two or three chapters on starting the young horse. I highly recommend you observe a good trainer and get some experience on the ground with him or her before you start your training program.

Understand and master identifying calmness.

Don't let fear or excitability get out of control.

Pit the horse's strength against himself. Don't match his strength against you. The horse has no business knowing he is stronger than you.

Spring is the time of year to start training the young horses that are around two years of age. The weather, for the most part, is better. I start all my young horses around two years of age with 90 days of ground work with limited riding. After the first 90 days I turn them back into the pasture until three years of age.

This training concept has worked wonders for me. When you start back at three, the horse's mind is quieter and is less likely to turn a minor infraction into a major crisis. You need to realize that in the first 90 days the horse is interested in his own self-preservation. In his mind he is not allowed to make any wrong steps in nature. He is working off his natural instincts.

One of the great things about starting your own horse is it gives you an opportunity to get to know yourself. If you are hot-tempered and quick to fly off the handle, you have no place in training a horse. You have to change your temperament, and thereby lower your blood pressure.

At the other end of the spectrum, if you are too kind-hearted you won't get the respect you need to train the horse. Try to strike a median between the two extremes. Set boundaries so the horse is respecting and trusting you as his leader and knows what is acceptable behavior and what is not acceptable behavior.

If your horse has not been handled you need to start with developing trust. One of the first things I do is put the colt in a stall and start feeding grain and hay once in the morning and once in the evening. An ear of corn at lunch really helps with shedding the caps of his baby teeth.

Some colts will be untamed and fearful of being touched. When this is the case, some trainers turn to a lariat to rope the horse and use a snubbing post to pull the horse up to the post and put the halter on. This is dangerous at best and does require skill in roping. Some trainers use a cutting gate to crowd the horse in the stall. This also is dangerous at best. Some trainers use Ace (a sedative drug) in the feed to sedate the horse in an attempt to get the halter on the horse. These shortcuts may work on some horses and may not on others. The bottom line is, if you are resorting to these crude methods you have not given enough time to gain the horse's trust.

Watch his behavior in the stall for the first couple of weeks. Is he flighty when you approach? Does he climb the walls when you open the stall door? Will he let you catch and pet him?

I'm not going to debate with you if you should leave him in the stall or turn him out in a paddock. That depends on your situation. The main thing is developing trust using a feeding schedule.

Your tasks now are to get the halter on the horse and get him to a place where he can be tied. Feed is a powerful motivator for horses and definitely a short cut you can take advantage of. Take the time it takes and don't get into a hurry. Most of the time you'll be able to

From the Trail to the Rail   13

calm and halter a colt with just this feeding program.

Stay at the feeding program for as long as it takes to get the job done. I've had a 98% success rate with the feeding program. Your horse will eventually eat from a bucket you're holding and let you start rubbing his neck. In no time you are friends.

Weaning your foal is a great time to apply our theory. Most farm-raised foals are gentle to work. However, you can occasionally have one that is higher strung or spoiled and these colts can be a challenge for anyone.

Mr. Picasso will assist us on our journey for his first 90 days of training. He has been kept up in the stall with daily turn out time as already described. He was fed consistently as a youngster in the field to develop trust in people. He is a young stallion with limited focus time, meaning he likes to think of areas of other adventures and play.

Every training situation (condition) is different. I recommend you turn the horse out after 90 days but that may not be the best plan in your situation. Stay with what works for you. The main points are to go slow and take your time with the young horse. Your horse will not develop his full strength and a mature mind until the age of four. This gives us two winters of work to get him ready for a lifetime of great trail work.

Every year I see good two-year-old horses in the show ring but seldom see the same horses back at three. Unfortunately, these horses were either hurt or their minds were blown. Remember, a two-year-old is a baby with a blank sheet of paper that becomes a three-year-old. The great thing about a three-year-old is he becomes four.

Now depending on the training situation, some folks can tie their horse first and some will have to teach leading first. A majority of folks are going have to teach the colt to lead in order to get him to a place to tie him. I use a strong halter with a 22-foot lead rope. Try to use a round pen or barn hallway so if the colt gets away he can't go far. The walls will come in handy in controlling the colt's movements. Do not wrap the lead rope around your hands and don't let the lead rope get tangled around your feet, for obvious reasons.

Stand to the side in front of the colt at a 45-degree angle. Now pull the colt sharply and stand him up facing you. Make him face you. Then go to the other side, stand at a 45-degree angle and sharply stand the colt up facing you. If the colt takes off and runs past you, just plant your feet and stand him up facing you sharply. When you do this about three or four good efforts you will notice the colt's feet start to free up and he will take a couple of steps toward you. Try to let him follow you on a slack lead rope. Everything we do needs to have a reward with a slack lead rope.

Do not tie the end of rope at this time to any fixed objects. Do not place anything but the halter around the colt's nose. Just keep working on leading on a slack lead rope. The colt will start to follow you and in a couple of hours you will be off to a great start. Remember, when you add pressure to the rope immediately release it as soon as the colt starts forward and tell him he is a good boy. Just keep at this pattern for as long as it takes. Your horse will get the message and start following you. As you start to teach these first few lessons don't forget to invite your equine training professional or other competent friend to assist you.

The first lessons of the rope and halter can provide some anxious moments when you tie the colt for the first time. The 'x' factor is you don't know how hard the colt will struggle against standing tied, but you can bet there will be a struggle. If you take care and see that he is properly tied it's unlikely he will hurt himself.

When I tie the colt for the first time I use a rubber inner tube tied about eight feet high on the side of the barn. Make sure you have a good strong rope and a heavy halter. Use a slipknot to tie at both ends, one at the inner tube, and the other at the halter. I tie both ends to make sure the horse stays tied and does not break a metal snap.

Let the lesson begin without you interfering. The colt needs to understand and work this out for himself. If the colt falls, untie him, let him get back to his feet, and tie him again. The colt needs to test the rope and halter and be convinced that it's stronger than he is and there is no use in pulling or struggling.

As soon as you are convinced that the colt knows to stand tied on a slack rope it's time to hard tie him to a solid object without the rubber inner tube. A strong barn post will keep the lesson of the rope in the colt's mind. It's important that you use a good quality halter and rope to prevent the colt from breaking free. Now it does happen, but if the colt breaks free it's not the end of the world. Just tie him back as quickly as possible. These lessons should start at 15 minutes in length and work up to 1 hour. Don't over stress your young horse.

Stay with the halter breaking and leading for a couple of months. Don't get in a hurry. Your goal is to get your horse to lead consistently on a slack rope.

When I was much younger I used to put the horse in a round pen and have him under saddle and ridden in less than two hours. I thought this was cutting edge training, but now I realize it is only flooding the horse and does not build a good foundation for a sound, calm mind. The time we use between the ages of two and four to develop the horse's mind is the key to success.

Review

Tasks: Spend your time establishing trust. Teach the horse to be caught and let you put on the halter. Teach the horse to lead on a slack rope and teach the horse to stand tied.

Conditions: The conditions under which you teach these lessons must be safe for you and the horse.

Standards: The standards are that the horse trusts you enough to allow you to catch and halter it easily; leads respectfully and consistently on a slack rope; and stands tied for up to one hour without fighting the tie rope.

Chapter Five: Controlling the Hindquarters

"To learn you have to listen, to improve you have to try." Unknown

Everything we've done so far has been working with the horse's head. In order to train the horse you have to get the horse to move his feet. Now this is going to sound strange, but to get control of the horse we have to shift our thinking to the hindquarters. Most people stay focused on the head with the halter, but make no mistake about it, to control the horse you have to control the hindquarters.

Before we think about riding we need to teach the young horse where to put his feet. More importantly, we need to watch and learn how he uses his feet and commit this to our long-term memory. Knowing how, when, and where the horse is going to move his feet will give us a definite advantage over the horse. We have to develop a system to control the horse's feet on the ground.

The oldest fundamental exercise known to man is rear-end under, front-end across. Early knights and other mounted warriors used this movement in battle to defend themselves.

There are many different names for the rear-end under movement. For example: Roll the hocks over, disengage the hindquarters, shut off the power, defuse the power, the list goes on and on. I use different names in this chapter for teaching purposes. This is to acquaint you with the different names to keep confusion at bay. I don't care what names you choose to call disengaging the hindquarters. Always remember this, rear-end under is a safety control you must understand first and foremost.

Learning rear-end under and front-end across is a requirement for all gaited horses and trainers to master. This movement will take us from the ground to upper level training.

Tasks:

(1) Rear-end under.

(2) Front-end across.

(3) Lunge to right and left.

(4) Cause the horse to back up.

(5) Put the dance together: Rear-end under, front-end across.

All we need is a rope halter and a 22-foot lead rope and a small 25-foot by 25-foot pen or similar enclosure to assist in controlling the young horse's movement. The 22-foot rope with the fence gives you enough slack to roll the hindquarters over and not be dragged around the pasture by the horse.

The first step in taking the power away from the colt is called disengaging the hindquarters. Stand on the left side of the horse and take the lead rope in your left hand.

You can use a riding crop, or the excess end of the lead rope, in your right hand. Put pressure on the horse's left hip, tapping towards his hip with your lead rope or riding crop.

You want the colt to cross his left hind leg over his right hind leg. Keep adding pressure until the colt gives you the cross over. When you get the inside hind leg to cross over make sure you reward the colt by releasing the pressure on the rope halter.

From the Trail to the Rail

Just keep building on this process. There should be no confusion here. Get this confirmed with the horse, meaning 100% trained and nothing less!

Now repeat this lesson while standing on the colt's right side, disengaging the hindquarters so the right hind leg crosses over in front of the left hind leg. Reward the colt by releasing pressure on the halter when he rolls over his hocks.

You have to teach both sides of the horse. Remember, a horse has two sides to his brain with an eye on each side. This is the reason why you can ride one way and every-thing is great, then ride back the same way going the other direction and the horse is scared to death of the mailbox you already passed. I do believe the horse is capable of independent thoughts. He can use both sides of his brain at the same time. This makes the horse much quicker in thought for self-preservation. He may be training with you on the left eye, but wanting to flee on the right eye. You have to teach the horse on both sides of his brain and both eyes.

Simply tying the horse correctly can help tremendously in teaching disengage-ment of the hindquarters. I like to use a 3-inch diameter, 10-foot long pipe ce-mented 3 feet in the ground with a truck axle placed on the top for tying the young horses. When you tie the colt he will go around in circles disengaging his hind-quarters, or taking the power away from himself.

From the Trail to the Rail   19

When you roll the hindquarters over the hocks, it gives you a much better chance to handle the horse's strength. You are now teaching the horse you are stronger. Never let the horse know he is stronger than you. I try to use the colt's strength against himself in such a way that he defeats himself. The good news here is you don't have be an Olympic weight lifter to be stronger than the horse, just get the horse's power from the hindquarters shut off. Disengage the horse's power by crossing his near hind leg over his off hind leg.

Just for fun, take your colt to a stand of trees. Let him walk off or pass through the trees. When the lead rope makes contact with a tree, your colt will roll his hindquarters over facing you. Now start watching for this rear-end under in everything you do with your horse. Recognize the movement as other people lead their horses. Watch advanced work under saddle with good riders on their horses. See the movement and become very familiar in recognizing the foot pattern. Watch your favorite Western movies and look for the foot pattern. Always remember this, rear-end under is a safety control.

Now that we have control of the hindquarters, it is time to bring the front-end across. Stand in front of your colt and hold the lead rope in your left hand. Use the excess lead rope or riding crop in the right hand to apply pressure on the left hip by moving towards the left hip. Use the crop or lead rope to assist in getting the colt to move around you to the left. As the colt comes around you, use your left hand to pick up on the lead rope to put pressure on the colt's face so the hindquarters roll over the hocks. Now change hands. Use your right hand to lift the lead rope, put pressure on the colt's face as the colt finishes his movement of rear-end under and ask him to walk off to the right.

Repeat this from the colt's right side. Stand in front of the colt holding the lead rope in your right hind. Use the crop or excess lead rope in your left hand to apply pressure to the colt's right hip, moving him in a circle around you to the right. As the colt comes around, use your right hand to put pressure on the rope so he disengages his hindquarters. Change hands so the rope is again in your left hand as the colt finishes the rear-end under and ask him to walk off to the left.

Some horses will understand the concept better if you break it down into two steps. After the rear-end rolls over from the left, stop for a few seconds. Then ask the horse to bring the front-end across going to the right.

All this sounds fine and very simple but there are a lot of things that can and will go wrong. Your colt is going to figure out pretty quick that you are attempting to control his hindquarters. He is no dummy and most horses don't want you there. When you go to the hindquarters the colt will try to turn and face you. Most of the time, he'll turn on his forehand just quick enough to keep facing you. I hold my arm up to act as a block in front of the horse's eye and then quickly put pressure on the hindquarters to make the colt go forward.

You should realize by now that you are also teaching the colt to lunge both ways, left and right. Get lunging 100% both ways, no gray areas. If you get it done now, it will not come back as a hole in the foundation later in the horse's training.

There are several ways to teach the colt to back up. The one you see most people teaching is to stand in front of the colt and shake the lead rope hard enough to agitate the horse, causing him to step backwards, then releasing for the reward.

Or you can stand in front of your colt, hold the lead with your left hand and use the excess rope in your right hand to swing back and forth in front of the horse's chest or front legs to cause him to take a step back. Remember to take the pressure off as soon as the colt takes a step backward.

Another way to teach the colt to back up is to stand in front of a gate with the colt on the other side. Shake the rope and slowly open the gate, giving a release for a reward when the colt steps backward. It doesn't matter what method you use as long as you teach the horse to step backwards and then reward him.

I can assure you that in the beginning when you start putting the dance together with rear-end under, front-end across, there will be lot of drag and pressure on the lead rope. To begin dancing with your colt, get the colt to lunge to the left by putting pressure on the horse's left hip. After a few circles, roll the rear-end under, change hands and ask for the front end across. Now make your horse lunge to the right for a few circles, then roll the rear-end under. Stop a few seconds, shake the rope, back the horse up a step or two and roll the front-end to the left. Just keep at it and in a couple of months the feel of the lead rope will get light and the dance begins.

Review: The tasks in this chapter are teaching rear-end under; teaching front-end across; teaching the horse to lunge to the right and left; teaching the horse to back up.

Conditions: A rope halter, a 22-foot lead rope, an enclosed pen or ring approximately 25 feet x 25 feet. A riding crop may be a useful aid.

Standards: The horse is 100% consistent about doing each task willingly with a light feel on the lead rope.

Chapter Six: Sacking Out

"Experience is a marvelous thing that enables you to recognize a mistake when you make it again." F. P. Jones

It's very important that you understand and have a good working knowledge of how to disengage the hindquarters as discussed in the previous chapter. Just stay in a holding pattern until you feel you and your horse are ready for this chapter. If you skipped starting there I highly recommend, for safety reasons, that you start at the beginning of this book and work through each chapter before continuing with your training program.

The only fast way to train a horse is slowly. Don't forget to refresh your memory of safety before, during, and after the training. Asking for help from your professional trainer or other competent friend is just good common horse sense.

Sacking out is a tough concept to put on paper to teach. What you're trying to accomplish is for the horse to accept scary objects without blowing a fuse. Now this is going to require that you discover just how much pressure you can put on the horse, then working calmly, add and take away pressure. Now here is the rub. You have to put some pressure on the horse to teach him to accept the scary object. You want the horse to show some anxiety but you must work within the limits of his anxiety to perceive how much pressure is enough but not too much. Recognize when the horse accepts the scary object and is calm in his mind and feet. When the horse accepts the object and you did not melt down his mind, you're on your way to producing a trusting, confident animal.

From the Trail to the Rail

If you put too much pressure on the horse and blow a fuse every time you start you can do more harm than good. There is no way you can improve on the old sayings, "How much does it take?" and "How little does it take?"

Using Mr. Picasso as our two-year-old subject we will proceed with demonstrating sacking out. I start by holding the lead rope in my right hand. I use a flag for the first few lessons. I can gauge the horse's reaction better and stay more in a safety zone where the horse can't bite, kick, strike, or run over the top of me.

Now you don't have to go out and buy a flagstick. Just use a riding crop around 36 inches long with a small plastic bag or a ribbon tied around the end. If the horse notices the flag in your right hand and shows a reaction, present the flag to him and let him inspect it and touch it with his nose. If the horse hollows his back, draws back and snorts just calmly hold the flag and follow him back towards the fence. Keep presenting it to him. You should stay calm and not overreact.

A round pen or small enclosure 24 feet x 24 feet will most certainly help. Keep the lead rope slack but keep the horse facing you while presenting the flag. Now here is how we can tell if the previous training has been effective. During the sacking out process some horses will bolt or attempt to go sideways to get away from the pressure. When the horse tightens the lead rope, hold firm, causing him to roll his rear-end under and disengage his hindquarters. Once you have confidence you can disengage the hindquarters by standing firm, the sacking out process become easier with other objects.

I use ropes, flags, tin cans, an umbrella, a cap pistol, a leaf blower, a plastic tarp, saddle blankets, and a light saddle. In your training program you can add and modify your own sack-out list. For most sacking out I try to sack out the air at the end of the lead rope and work my way towards the horse. Go slowly at first, and then move with natural movements. When I start getting close to the colt I use the 3-second rule. What I mean is I only present the scary object for three seconds then remove it from the horse.

For example, let's take an umbrella. With the horse facing you, stand at the end of the lead rope. Open and close the umbrella while at the end of the lead rope. Move off at a 45-degree angle from the horse's right eye, then arc back to a 45-degree angle from the colt's left eye.

Keep moving back and forth at 45-degree angles, opening and closing the umbrella. Study the horse's reactions and level of anxiety at this distance. Keep in mind, you have to have some level of anxiety in order to teach the hoorse to accept the umbrella. When you get within arm's reach of the horse's nose let the horse smell and touch the umbrella, but for only 3 seconds, then remove it from his touch. Be careful with the tip of the umbrella. I tape a soft cloth over the sharp end.

The idea is you need to know when the horse's fear turns to curiosity. Most horoses will start looking for the scary umbrella. When presenting the umbrella watch to see if there is a big stretch forward with his neck to investigate the umbrella. Build on the colt's curiosity. Walk towards the horse's nose, present the umbrella, count - thousand one, thousand two, thousand three, then step back away from the colt. You and the horse both need to recognize that danger came and danger left, the same as pressure on, pressure off or turning the volume up, turning the volume down. Get a handle on these concepts when sacking out your horse.

If everything has gone well it's time to introduce the saddle blanket and saddle. Roll the horse's rear-end under and have the horse facing you. Stand with the lead rope in your left hand and the saddle blanket in your right hand. Present the blanket to the colt. Let the horse smell the blanket for 3 seconds then remove the blanket from his face. Go back and forth with the blanket just getting the horse used to the movement of 3 seconds in and 3 seconds out. When the horse accepts the blanket and is calm you can start swinging the blanket freely onto his back, then off his back. The thing to remember here is to establish a rhythm, back and forth. Just keep working until the blanket doesn't mean anything. Do not hit the horse too hard as to sting him, hurting him with it will teach him to be afraid of it. Now use the blanket like a towel, or just get a bath towel, and rub the colt all over his body. Place the blanket on the horse's back just like you were going to put on the saddle. Let the horse pack the blanket as you lead him.

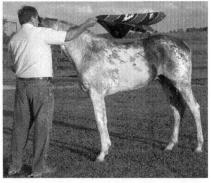

After the horse calmly accepts the saddle blanket stand beside your colt on the left side, place the excess lead rope around the horse's back and wrap it under his belly to imitate a belly strap. Pull slightly tight and watch for the colt's reaction. Do this several times per session. It will pay dividends when putting on the saddle girth.

The first time I put a saddle on the horse I use a light saddle that I can handle with one hand. Hold the horse with your left hand and place the saddle on the horse's back. with your right hand. Carefully reach under the horse's belly and secure the girth. Now you're going to tie or buckle the girth for the first time. I recommend you only tighten it enough to hold the saddle in place.

It is very important that you turn the horse loose and watch his reaction. Some horses will explode trying to get the saddle off. Other horses will walk off in a calm manner wearing the saddle. Now don't panic if your horse tries to buck off the saddle. It most certainly does not mean your sacking out program is not working. Remind yourself what would happen if you had not done any sacking out prior to the first saddling. What happens here is the girth is tightened. The colt has to deal with continuous tight pressure around his belly, and this can cause violent reactions in some horses. The good news is once the horse understands that the girth pressure is not hurting him and is not going to go away the horse calms down very quickly. After two or three times of sacking out with the saddle most horses walk around in a calm manner. Your horse will seldom repeat his first episode.

As the sacking out process continues I highly recommend you put the saddle on every day for a couple of weeks. Use the saddle leather stirrups to help sack out the horse on his side. Now don't crucify him, just let him know that the stirrup leathers won't hurt him. Make some popping noises with the stirrup leathers against the saddle panels. Get the horse standing still and accepting the saddle. Then use your flag to rub all over the saddle.

For most horses sacking out will continue just fine, following normal patterns of behavior getting the horse calm and accepting scary objects.

Every now and then you find a certain disposition in a horse that will resist you touching or using any sacking out method. Most of the time it is a high-headed stallion, this particular colt's attitude is, "Who do you think you are, rubbing my face and ears?" This colt has a "Don't touch me!" attitude which goes right down to his feet. When you go to rub this type of colt with your hand he pulls back or turns his head sideways. Now this colt can show different combinations of this behavior to avoid or resist training. Stand to the near (left) side, hold the colt with your left hand, and slowly rub the colt's neck with the goal of working towards his face and ears. If the colt moves, disengage his hindquarters and continue rubbing his neck. Stay in the horse's comfort zone moving only towards the face and ears when you have the green light of a calm mind. Work in tiny increments, getting the colt to accept your rubbing on his face and ears. I have had some colts take a long time to let you into their world. Remember to take the time it takes to get the job done.

When teaching a young horse everything you do is extremely important. Now sometimes what you don't do is just as important. I use a flagstick when starting the sacking out of the feet. Using a flagstick gives you time to read the horse's disposition and keeps you out of the kick zone. Start as explained earlier, just rubbing the horse with the flagstick. Most horses will accept the flagstick. Work around and down the feet teaching the horse that nothing is going to hurt him.

Read this carefully. If you encounter a horse that shows aggression and is willing to fight when you attempt to flag his feet, and despite all your attempts the horse still is aggressive, you need to stop before you teach the horse how to be more aggressive and pick up bad habits. Striking or pawing at the flag could eventually lead to aggressive behavior toward you. It's been my experience that a horse that is aggressive will also reach down and around and bite at the flagstick. You do not want to teach him how to square up and face you with two lethal weapons and a mouth! This horse is protecting himself the only way he knows how.

Whipping a frightened horse is foolish and only adds to the problem. Even professional football teams have to punt occasionally. Now is the time to call your equine professional or competent friend to help you through this valley. He or she will have several options available for them to work through the problem. The matter should resolve itself rather quickly with a professional. Sit back and watch your professional friend and take this opportunity to learn about you and your horse.

Review

Tasks: Teach the horse to calmly accept scary objects such as a flag stick, umbrella, saddle blanket, saddle, etc.

Conditions: You are still working the horse in a small pen using the halter and a 22-foot lead rope described in previous chapters. Be careful to stay in the colt's safety zones. Present each object, one thing at a time, using the 3-second rule of pressure on, pressure off, until the horse becomes curious and calmly accepts the scary objects. You are working in the horse's anxiety zone so pay careful attention to the horse's response. He will tell you how much pressure is enough and how much pressure is too much. Sacking out should never hurt, terrorize, or intimidate the horse.

Standards: The horse remains calm and stands quietly on a slack lead rope while the flag stick, umbrella, saddle blanket, or other object is moved around and over him, including his head and legs. These lessons may need to be reviewed occasionally throughout the colt's training.

Chapter 7: First Obstacle
More Sacking Out and the Obstacle Course

"If you do the little jobs well, the big one tends to take care of themselves."
Dale Carnegie

Some of the information from previous chapters I have repeated over and over again. Now I don't do this to insult your intelligence. There are many different situations and problems you may get into with your horse. It is impossible for me to cover all the things that might go wrong while training a horse in just three or four chapters. What I'm trying to do is stress some training points that will assist you in becoming successful.

When you have the ability to disengage the hindquarters and take the power away from the horse you most certainly have a good chance for successful training. You must understand that he who controls the hind-quarters controls the horse. A master teacher/trainer knows when, where, and how the horse is going to move his feet before the horse takes the first step. This is a powerful teaching tool that will pay you high training dividends. Gaining this experience or feel is most certainly within your reach. You have to be aware and observe your horse's feet leaving the ground. Start with rear-end under, front-end across, then build on your observations and apply the concept to daily training. Separate the front end from the back end. Get a good baseline of experience (feel) that you can build upon. Watch what happens with your horse's feet when things go right. Also watch what happens when things don't go according to plan.

The horse needs to be taught a step-up cue. Position the horse beside a rail or barn wall, holding the lead rope in your left hand. I use a 36 inch, stiff buggy whip to reach the horse's hindquarters. This keeps you from having to lean and be off balance when the whip causes the horse to activate the hindquarters. It stands to reason you will have to sack out the horse with the buggy whip first.

Tap the horse on the rump with the whip until you get one step forward. As soon as the horse steps forward stop tapping and release all pressure. Wait a few seconds then do it again. Tap one step forward, stop and release. When you get one-step forward on cue 100% of the time, meaning no gray area, the horse is trained. Then you can develop this so the horse takes two and three steps forward. Remember to watch and observe the horse's feet. Never forget the more you understand how horse's feet move the better trainer you become!

Try to stay ahead of the horse, observing his feet before and after each request. Determine how successful your predictions are before and after the horse's feet leave the ground. Just for fun, during an hour lesson period keep a score of how many hits and misses you have in observing the horse's footfall. Set a high goal of 100% predictability on how the horse is going to move his feet. It doesn't matter what lesson you're teaching, observe the horse's feet. Now if you get a range of 70% correct, that's a very respectable score.

I would recommend that you now put the saddle on the horse while sacking out, at least three or four times a week. This just gives the horse more time to accept his training.

I introduce the bit over the halter at about this time, but I do not attach the lead rope to the bit. At first I use no reins attached to the bit at all. I place the bit over the halter. I don't put the bit so high it wrinkles the corners of the horse's mouth. I want the horse to lift and hold the bit in his mouth.

Now you can continue sacking out lessons using a plastic tarp. Take a plastic tarp 10 feet by 12 feet and fold the tarp into a small 16 inch by 16 inch square. Tack your horse with the saddle and rope halter. Roll the rear-end under and have the horse stand facing you. You stand about 15 feet from the horse. Let the horse look at the plastic tarp and gauge his reaction or anxiety level. Adjust your movements to fit the situation. Wave the tarp around and over your head. Be a cheerleader. Walk toward the horse's face and count thousand one, thousand two, thousand three, then back away a few feet. Move back toward the horse using the same procedure. Let the horse smell and touch the plastic tarp. See if the horse stretches his neck forward to touch and smell the plastic tarp. This is when fear turns to curiosity. Most of the time, you can get this done within three seconds. Did you observe the horse's feet? Did you have to disengage the horse's hindquarters?

Repeat the same procedure but this time unfold the plastic tarp one fold. Now each time we go through this procedure the plastic tarp will get bigger. Stay at the sacking out pattern until the plastic tarp is completely unfolded to its full 10 feet by 12 feet. When you start waving the final unfolded plastic tarp around it may take some time for the horse to accept this lesson. Just remain calm and keep working. If your horse is continually overreacting fold the plastic tarp back up a few folds and stay there until you can proceed. Don't forget to work within the limits of the horse's anxiety and ability to accept the lesson. Pay attention to how the horse's feet are moving. Even if the lesson does not go well, you are getting great practice of disengaging the hindquarters and observing the feet.

Go back and fold the plastic tarp back into a 16-inch by 16-inch square. This time hold the horse with your left hand and rub the plastic

tarp all over the horse's near (left)side, neck, and body. Swap hands on the lead rope, step to the off (right)side and continue rubbing the horse's neck and body. Get him used to the different feel of the plastic. Observe the horse's feet and how he reacts to the sacking out. Then unfold the plastic tarp one fold and continue. Keep proceeding until the horse is standing under the plastic tarp just like a horse blanket. Be careful when the plastic tarp is completely unfolded that you don't trip or fall. Never forget the safety tips when sacking out your horse.

Since we have been using a plastic tarp, our first ground obstacle should be directing the horse to step onto and over the plastic tarp. Tack your horse with a saddle and rope halter. Spread the plastic tarp out on the ground. Again we must think of controlling the hindquarters and directing the horse from the hindquarters forward.

Now it's going to be a tough lesson if you think you can lead the horse straight across the tarp the first time. With most horses you end up trying to pull the horse across the plastic tarp. Some horses will let you lead them anywhere because they have a calm trusting mind but this is not the norm. We are sacking out and working towards getting a calm mind.

Before asking the horse to walk across the tarp you need to be able to lunge your horse both ways.

Position the horse about three or four feet from the plastic tarp obstacle. Stand off to the left side of your horse with the lead rope in your left hand. Tap the horse on the rump with a whip for the step forward cue. When the horse gives you one step towards the plastic tarp release, and reward the horse. Ask for another step-up cue, when you get the step towards the plastic tarp release and reward.

You're going to come to a point and time when the horse gives you a refusal and does not want to step forward towards the plastic. Now don't panic, just ask for another step-up cue. Observe if the horse drops his head, lifts his foreleg, or paws at the plastic. These responses mean that the horse is thinking of stepping forward so release and reward the horse. The horse is now testing where he can put his feet safely. We have to perceive this as an effort to please us. Keep asking with the step-up cue and the horse will eventually take a step onto the plastic.

I wish it could always go as smoothly as outlined above but with most young horses you will encounter two-year-old behavior. Some horses will pitch a fit, veering off to the side with a crow hop. You will get some horses that go backwards very quickly. Some horses will jump across the tarp with one stride. This is one of the reasons we stand and direct from the side, so the horse won't jump over the top of us. He can still veer off sideways over the top of you.

I find many horses that will look for an escape route between you and the obstacle. If you close the escape route too quickly the horse is very capable of running over the top of you. I would recommend that for this first obstacle you have your equine professional or competent friend work the horse while you watch him or her. This would be a great time to observe the feet. Watch to see how many times the hindquarters are disengaged. Determine if it's a good crossover with the hindquarters or a crow hop. A crow hop in the rear is not disengaging the hindquarters.

The first trailer load will follow the same pattern as the plastic tarp on the ground. Trailer loading is nothing more than good leading and obstacle play. The bottom line is when you have a trailer loading problem you have a leading problem. The problem will never resolve itself with forced trailer loading. The key is to direct your horse into the trailer from the ground controlling the hindquarters. The steps outlined above are the same training procedures for trailer loading.

Review: The tasks are teaching the horse to wear a saddle, teaching the horse to wear a bit, teaching the horse to step forward one step at a time on cue, sacking the horse out with a tarp and teaching the horse to walk across the tarp when it is spread out on the ground.

Conditions: Continue working in the small pen with the halter and 22-foot lead rope on the horse. Add a light weight saddle, and a snaffle bit with no reins. You will need a 36 inch long stiff buggy whip to teach the step up-cue. For sacking out you'll need a 10 foot by 12 foot plastic tarp.

Standards: The horse stands still and calm for saddling and accepts having the girth tightened without any fuss or protest. The horse accepts having you put the bridle on and will pick up and hold the bit quietly in its mouth. The horse steps forward one step every time you give it the step-up cue, either with a saddle or without. The horse remains calm and stands quietly on a slack lead rope when rubbed with the tarp and when the tarp is waved around him or placed on him. The horse walks calmly across the tarp when it is spread out on the ground.

Chapter Eight: Ground Driving

"It's up to us to explain (to the colt) what we expect when we are near. If we don't they will simply never know." Mark Rashid

Chapters One through Seven are getting us ready for ground driving. Please review these chapters and have a good working knowledge of disengaging the hindquarters and observing the colt's feet. If you have encountered problems with the previous training please resolve the matter before continuing with driving and riding concepts. A good equine professional or competent friend to assist you at this stage of training is good horse sense, especially if it's your first time driving a colt. The value of paying for private lessons and quality help cannot be overstated.

The reason I like to spend time ground driving prior to riding is ground driving gives us time to teach the colt to listen to the bit and follow his nose. We can teach a system of control (starting, turning, and stopping) on the ground safely.

Tack your colt with a saddle and place the bridle over the halter. A good lunging halter with side rings is a good choice to use if you have one available. No reins attached to the bit, just let the colt hold the bit in his mouth while going forward. I use two 22-foot, ½ inch cotton ropes for driving lines.

Words of caution, make sure the halter fits the colt. A loose halter can slip around and hurt the side of the colt's face and eyes. I use a small paddock to start my driving lessons. I highly recommend you use a round pen or other small 24 foot by 24 foot enclosure to start the first few driving lessons.

During the first few lessons when the outer line touches the hocks some colts overreact and get nervous. If the colt gets going too fast don't  overreact just give him some slack in both lines. The paddock walls will contain his movement, providing you are using a small enough paddock. Giving some slack will prevent you from being dragged from behind. Let the driving lines slip through your hands when needed. Using this method you can use the inside line and make the circle smaller to slow the colt.

If your sacking out work has been good and the colt stands still while you move around him you can probably get by without an assistant. For your benefit for the first few lessons it is helpful to have an assistant, what I call a header, hold the horse.

Think about coordinating and holding the driving lines in your hands.

From the Trail to the Rail

Do not wrap the lines around your hands or let excess driving lines get tangled around your feet.

Notice, I do not run the inside driving line through the stirrup. I use the inside line just the same way as we started working the colt on the ground. It should be obvious, the reason we start with the halter or lunging halter is to protect the colt's mouth. His heart and soul is located in his mouth so take care not to spoil his mouth, especially if you want him to walk off his hindquarters later.

Stand just like you have been when lunging the colt with the rope halter. Get the colt moving around you to the right. The right line is attached to the halter straight to your right arm, not through the stirrups leather. The left line is attached to the left side of the halter with the line running through the left stirrup, around the hocks, to your left hand. Ask the colt to move off to the right at a walk.

Most of the time, he will move out quickly. Now don't panic, you can slow him down by feeding line out so the walls will contain him. Making the circle smaller with the inside rein can slow the colt. You can use the outside rein to tip his nose toward the wall or fence. Don't forget to give a release when he slows down.

Now comes the hard part, you're going to have to teach him to stop. For the first few times I turn him into the rail and say "whoa." I use the outside line, in this case the left line, to turn the colt into the fence rail and roll his hindquarter over to the right. You should  be standing behind the colt. Make sure you are far enough behind to stay out of the kick zone. If he tries to move out again turn him back facing into the fence and say "whoa." Just as soon as the feet stop moving I release the line for a reward. If he starts going too fast when lunging and you can't control him, turn him loose. There is no sense what so ever for you to be dragged around the paddock or feel some rope burns.

The reason we tack and drive the colt this way is get some experience, feel, and not hurt the colt. Practice starting and stopping the colt until you become comfortable with this procedure. Keep in mind you are going to have to approach the colt to make adjustments. Stop the colt on the fence as stated. Use either hand to roll the rear end under for a 180-degree turn around. The colt now will be facing you, his rump in front of the fence. Say "whoa." Remember to give plenty of slack to complete the turn and a release for the reward.

From the Trail to the Rail   33

The next day start the lesson on the left eye and work through the same method going to the left. Attach the driving lines so that the left line is attached to the halter, straight to your left hand, not through the left stirrup. Attach the right rein to the right side of the halter with the line running through the right stirrup, around the hocks, to your right hand. Ask the colt to move off to the left at a walk.

When you're ready, after getting the colt comfortable with this method, place each line through the stirrups. Caution! Don't step within kicking range behind the colt. Just slightly move to rear of the colt, out of kicking range, and practice the same method. After a few rounds stop the colt then move behind the colt, staying out of kicking range, and continue with the lesson.

Now you can start your turns to the left and right. Turn your colt to the left into the fence just like you were going to stop but don't stop, just roll the hindquarters over the hocks 180 degrees and continue driving. Don't forget to give a release (reward) for a complete request.

It is very important to let the colt stretch his head down and relax. I can almost assure you some colts will not want to stretch down into the halter and round their top line. Just stay the course until the colt drops his head. It may take some time but most will eventually reach out and drop their neck and head into the halter. This is so important for future training.

Coordinating the driving lines is a subject that has to be discussed before we attach reins to the bit. For right now you need be able give slack with your hands and take up slack with your hands. To feed out slack just relax your hands and let the rope slide, giving the colt more freedom. There is nothing sissy about using a pair of gloves until you get used to driving. To gather up the drive reins I use my fingers, gently crawling like a spider and gathering line as I go. I don't try to hold the excess line, I just let it feed through my hands to the ground.

Just for practice, have a friend hold the ends of the driving lines. Take up a line in each hand. To take out slack of the lines just let the rope slide out of your hands. Your friend can take a step away from you. To gather up the slack, walk gently with your fingers gathering the line taking out slack. When you first start to drive on the ground there will have be some give and take on your part. The colt is trying figure out what you want so just be steady with the lines. Never forget you can put a tremendous amount of pressure in the colt's mouth if you're not careful and spoil the colt's mouth.

When I was in Officer Candidate School, the Senior Tact Officer's favorite words were practice, practice and practice. This was preached day in and day out, most of the time twenty hours a day. I graduated as a Second Lieutenant with those words burned into my memory. The word still haunts me today if I don't apply it to colt training.

I use a full cheek rubber coated snaffle bit and stay with this bit until I get the colt following his nose, turning and stopping consistently. Now here is where I differ from the conventional wisdom. I put the bridle on the colt over the halter as described. I use a zip tie to connect around the halter ring and bit ring on both sides. I now snap the driving lines onto the zip ties. This is just one more step in protecting the mouth. The colt is used to the reins being snapped to the halter. The zip ties will ensure an add safety feature prior to snapping the lines directly to the bit.

Start driving the colt, the only thing different is feed both lines through their respective saddle stirrups. Take the driving reins in each hand. Get the colt to follow his nose. Do a lot of turns, starting and stopping.

Pay particular attention to the colt's mouth. Is he gaping his mouth open? Is his tongue hanging out? Is he tossing his head from side to side? Most of these reactions are signs of resistance. The immediate measure you can take is to let off the pressure, use slack lines. More than likely you did not see any resistance signs until you snapped onto the bit so you can bet the farm you've got too much pressure in the colt's mouth. Back off with heavy hands and work more on loose slack lines. In time the colt's mouth will calm. Try to see how little pressure it takes to turn the colt. See if you turn the colt to the left or right with only the weight of a fly landing on the lines. Determine how little pressure it takes to stop the colt. See if you can just tip his outside eye into the fence or wall and get a soft stop. When you are finished with the day's lesson gently roll the rear end under and get the colt to face you.

When working with long lines on the colt don't dally around when the lesson is finished. Go directly to the colt and unsnap the driving reins from the bit. Put the colt up and let him think about the day's lesson.

When the colt is driving to standards with no signs of resistance in the mouth it is time to leave off the halter and snap the reins directly onto the bit. It should be an easy step for the colt. Please remember to be careful. Don't dull the colt's mouth. Review all safety points.

Review

Tasks: Teach the colt to ground drive: Starting, walking, turning, and stopping, first with just the halter, then with a snaffle bit.

Conditions: Continue working in the 25 foot x 25 foot pen. You'll need the halter, saddle, and two 22-foot long ½ inch cotton ropes for driving lines (reins). After the colt has learned to ground drive in the halter add a rubber coated, full cheek snaffle bit. Attach the driving lines to zip ties between the bit and halter rings the first few times you drive with a bit.

Standards: The colt should walk calmly with his head low, turn in both directions in response to light pressure on the driving lines, and stop and stand in response to the command "whoa" and light pressure, all without gaping his mouth, hanging his tongue out, or resisting the bit.

Chapter Nine: First Ride

"Before everything else, getting ready is the secret of success." Henry Ford

All the training steps thus far are building blocks for the first ride. For safety reminders please review all the previous chapters. I don't believe you have to be a professional rider to give the colt his first ride. I think you must be calm and relaxed and have confidence in the saddle. You should be able to mount and dismount without stressing your colt. You do not want to cause your colt to move because you do not have the upper body strength to get on quickly.

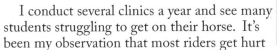

I conduct several clinics a year and see many students struggling to get on their horse. It's been my observation that most riders get hurt getting on or off the horse. Although our method of training minimizes a lot of problems on the part of colt, I can't guarantee there won't be some quick jumps or crow hopping.

If you aren't sure that you have the confidence, strength, or balance to deal with anything the colt might do there is no shame in having a professional or competent friend ride the colt for the first few rides. Look at it this way, the shame is on you if you do not have someone help you when you or the colt need it. If the colt has been properly sacked out and the colt's mind is calm there will be little reaction from the colt's point of view.

Two things I do prior to riding the colt are: 1. Introduce him to the mounting block; and 2. Introduce him to human live weight.

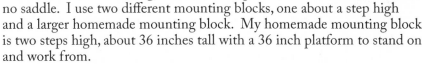

The mounting block, if used properly, is a great tool. The older I get the more I appreciate its usefulness. I start these lessons on the ground with a rope halter with no saddle. I use two different mounting blocks, one about a step high and a larger homemade mounting block. My homemade mounting block is two steps high, about 36 inches tall with a 36 inch platform to stand on and work from.

I do not advocate you carry mounting blocks around the National Forests to mount or dismount your horse. If you think about it, the trails are full of natural mounting blocks. I do recommend you carry one in the back of your truck. You don't need a mounting block to train a colt if you are young and athletic. A good mounting block makes life a little easier for the folks that have spent twenty plus years in the factory. The mounting block is nothing more than a tool.

You must consider safety when getting the colt prepared to work around a mounting block. Exposing your horse to having a rider work above his head is good sacking out prior to riding. The upper level trifocal vision in the horse's eyes is being sacked out. This is where the high-headed, full throttled, flight mode button is located.

Place a rope with a slip ring around the colt's neck. Make sure the noose is around the neck behind the poll. Hold the colt in your left hand put the small-step mounting block on the colt's left side. When standing on the mounting block watch your footing so you won't fall. Don't let the colt swing into you or the mounting block and knock you off balance. Rub the colt with your right hand. It's just sack out time. What you want to know is if the colt will stand still and doesn't move while you are standing over him at this height.

If he moves away, step off the mounting block at the near (left) side then stand him up very sharply facing you. Go to the off (right) side and stand him up again very sharply. There is no gray area. The colt must learn to stand still. He will if you will use a firm attitude.

Place the small-step mounting block on the near side of the colt. Hold the colt with your left hand. Bounce up and down about three small jumping efforts, just like you were preparing to mount with your foot in stirrup. If the colt moves stand him up sharply both sides. Be determined and firm.

When the colt is used to your bouncing up and down, still holding the rope in your left hand, also grab a firm grip of mane. Use this same rhythm to bounce up and lay across the colt's back. While you are lying on your stomach across the colt's back pet him on the off side with your free hand.

Now go to the off side (right) and repeat the same procedure. Get the colt used to live weight on his back. You can use a helper to hold the colt while you roll on and off his back. It stands to reason the helper needs to have a good working knowledge of disengaging the colt's hindquarters.

Tack the colt with the saddle and halter only. Just turn the colt loose in a small paddock or round pen, let him feel the saddle. Let the colt play at liberty getting rid of excess energy. When he's calm and ready to stand quietly, catch and hold the colt with your left hand and pop the saddle flaps with your right hand. Then move to the off side and pop the saddle flaps. This should be old school now and cause no movement or overreaction from the colt.

Place the bridle on the colt and have him stand between the fence and the two-step mounting block. Spend some time on the first step just rubbing the colt on the neck. Talk quietly with a soothing voice. Now move to top of the mounting block. Let the colt see you at this height. Read his reactions.

When the colt is perfectly calm go ahead and place your foot into the stirrup and mount the colt. Most of the time the colt will stand still. You use this time to get your other foot in the stirrups. Don't panic and nudge him with your heels. If he bolts forward it is no big deal. Moving forward is what you want in the long run. I like the old timer's saying, "Stay in the saddle and keep the horse between you and the ground."

There is nothing wrong with having a helper lead you for the first few rides. Just sit on the colt and let him get used to live weight. Don't forget about the mounting block and let the colt run into it or over the top of it. The helper can remove the mounting block out of the way.

Most gaited horses do not buck on the first ride. More than likely he does not have enough balance to buck with you on the first ride. About the fourth ride the colt has lost his fear of being mounted and may try to challenge your authority with a crow hop or buck or two. Just ride him forward quickly out of the notion.

Riding a horse forward can and will solve a lot of problems. Why? He has not picked up any bad habits or become confirmed in any nasty horse behavior. If your colt wants to suck the ground with his nose, keep his head about even with his withers and push him forward. You can now say your colt is green started. Now that does not mean he will not crow hop or shy when startled. You need to realize he has the right to make mistakes. How else is he going to learn?

In training a young horse you are going to make mistakes, so does everybody else. The difference between a young trainer and a professional trainer is the number of mistakes made and the ability to read the horse. A good professional trainer had to start as a novice. The key is to train under the supervision of a competent trainer.

Now if you are training a horse that has learned some bad habits it will require a different approach than driving him forward, which can make matters worse. Using a professional trainer or competent friend to help you with re-training a horse with bad habits is good common horse sense. When re-starting a horse go back to the first steps of this method to gain trust and work through each chapter to develop a trusting mind in the horse.

When I use the words "professional" and "competent," I use a strict dictionary interpretation of the words. It's been my experience that all good trainers have one thing in common. They all have a different way of saying the same things.

In chapters one through eight it was my intent to show you a system that would give you and your colt the confidence to start him under saddle for the first ride. Developing a sound and trusting mind between the ages of two to four years is like fine wine, it takes time. Now I'm sure you could have trained much faster with quicker results. Ask yourself this question: Are the results up to standards? Does the horse have a calm trusting mind?

Some trainers go much faster. To them I can only say, why not train slowly? The 2-year-old and 3-year-old colts are not mentally or physically strong enough to carry you over the trails. Take advantage of the time to train for a calm and trusting mind. When your colt turns four he will be strong enough to graduate quietly to the trail or rail.

You are the one who is responsible for building confidence in the colt's mind. It is you who has to set the standards. Good training is not a grasshopper application of training today then missing a week. Try to train at least three or four times a week, preferably four days in a row, then let the colt rest soak (think about it).

The difficult part about colt training is knowing when to add pressure and when to take away pressure. Even if you make mistakes, stay with sacking out and ground work for as long as it takes to get the results of a calm and trusting colt.

Review

Tasks: Teach the colt to accept a mounting block; get the colt used to mounting and dismounting; get the colt used to having live weight on his back; and ride the colt for the first times.

Conditions: Continue working in the paddock or pen you've been using for ground training. Have a safe, portable mounting block that you can bring into the pen to use for teaching the colt to stand still beside it. Saddle the colt, but use the halter only for the first ride. Remember, he can't go very far or very fast in a 25 foot x 25 foot paddock.

Standards: The colt will stand perfectly still and remain calm while you mount and dismount from either side using a mounting block or when you mount directly from the ground. The colt remains standing until you tell him to move, then walks forward calmly and quietly on loose reins.

Chapter Ten: Understanding Pace and Trot

"We never do anything well 'til we cease to think about the manner of doing it." William Hazlitt

When training our gaited horse it stands to reason we need to have a working knowledge and understanding of the different gaits a horse will exhibit in his movements. Tennessee Walking Horses, Missouri Fox Trotters, Rocky Mountain Horses, and Racking Horses are all very popular horse breeds you find on the trails. Ever wonder what the difference between a gaited horse breed and non-gaited horse breed is? Several good books have been written on this subject but there still remains an extreme amount of confusion regarding the difference. The best way to remember the difference is the gaited horse has the ability to add speed to the walk.

When you ride a nice western pleasure Quarter Horse and add speed to the walk, nine times out of ten the horse will go into a trot. Keep adding speed to the trot more than likely you'll get a lope. This horse does not have the ability to add gaited speed to the walk.

When you go to a harness racing track and watch the pacing horses add speed to the walk nine times out of ten they will pace. Keep adding speed more than likely you will pace the horse into a gallop. Again, this horse does not have ability to add gaited speed to the walk.

In the equine world at one end of a scale is a diagonal horse and the other end of the scale is a lateral horse. Using the same scale our gaited horses fall between the trot and the pace, doing what we identify as middle gaits. The running walk, fox trot, and a self-carriage walk are found in the middle gaits. In training our gaited horses the middle gaits are what we want to teach as the standard for our specific breeds. Now here is where the confusion hits us. Your gaited horse is multi-gaited, meaning he can perform all the aforementioned gaits in less than ten strides. To make matters even more confusing he can add speed within each variation of footfall.

Gait Scale		
Diagonal feet move together	Feet move separately and evenly timed	Lateral feet move together
Trot	◄faster slower►	**Flat Walk**	◄slower faster►	**Pace**
	Fox Trot	**Running Walk**	**Stepping Pace**	
		Rack		
Tendency to trot is called "too square" and may connect with a muscular weakness in the hindquarters		Tendency to pace is called "too slick" and may connect with a muscular weakness in the back

When your gaited horse is born his gait is pure in movement. These pure movements are easy to observe and will stay for approximately two to three weeks. Then the foot fall patterns will move into the gait scale of mixing and matching. Now all of this sounds technical but it's not.

When I use the term gaited-speed I'm referring to the horse's ability to add speed to the walk, separating his feet evenly. I think a square gait is using one leg at a time with independent movement of each leg separating into an evenly time four-beat step. The horse moves one-quarter step at a time with each leg. He has the ability to add speed while keeping his feet evenly timed. Now the problem comes in when the horse adds speed to the walk and drifts toward the pace or trot.

We have identified two major gaits using a scale, the trot (diagonal) and pace (lateral). What we want to teach our trail horses are middle gaits. Now depending on which breed we ride, the finished gait will be a running walk, a fox trot, a self-carriage walk, or a rack. The Walking Horse, Missouri Fox Trotter, Rocky Mountain Horse, and Racking Horse all have the middle gaits in common and believe it or not, most are able to perform all the gaits at any given time.

Let's try to get some definitions and understanding of how the gaited horse uses his feet to assist us in identifying the leg movements. Remember from previous chapters I can't overstate how important it is for you to work with the horse's feet.

Let's start at each end of the scale, the right side is lateral/pace, the left side is diagonal/trot, and work towards the middle which we can define as a flat walk with the respective breeds.

Let's develop a simple numbering system to aid in identifying gaits. Start counting the feet with the left hind foot (leaving the ground) as number 1, the left front foot (leaving the ground) as number 2, the right hind foot (leaving the ground) as number 3, and the right front foot (leaving the ground) as number 4. Now it really doesn't matter where you start the count. The feet always move in the same sequence. For example, start

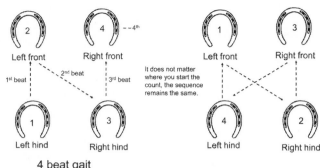

4 beat gait

the left forefoot as number 1, then the right rear as number 2, the right forefoot as number 3, the left rear as number 4. When the horse takes four steps it is one stride. The following is one stride of a natural walk and any other four-beat gait.

Left rear<1> Left front<2> Right rear<3> Right front<4>

The pace is a two-beat gait. The horse uses both legs on the same side, often referred to as the lateral pair, working together and leaving the ground together at the same time, shifting his weight from side to side. In our number system feet one and two are one beat on the left side, feet three and four are one beat on the right side. The feet are working together as one unit creating a two-beat gait. Watch closely and you can see the front foot and rear foot leave the ground at the same time. The lateral pace is a rough gait to ride. You will feel a side-to-side shift in the saddle. The horse's head will remain high and stiff most of the time. The horse that is capable of race track pacing speeds has a moment of suspension, or fly time, when all four feet are off the ground. In today's gaited world, when you hear the term, "the horse is too slick," it means

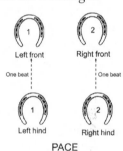

PACE

nothing more than too pacey. Now don't get wrapped around the axle. The pace can be a tool or a problem depending on how we use the tool. Now I've always heard in the gaited horse world, "No pace, no walk." I have come to find this is a very true statement. When you find a good flat walk you find a hint of the pace in the gait, just as you will find a hint of the trot.

When you first start training a pacey horse or re-training a performance horse to a light-shod horse you will get very frustrated with the pace. During my clinics I spend more time with students solving pace problems than in any other area of the clinic. The pace will be discussed in more detail later in the problem-solving chapters.

The trot is also a two-beat gait. The horse uses the diagonal legs together, which is the difference from the pace. When the left front foot and the right hind foot leave the ground together as a unit creating

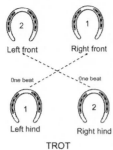

Left front   Right front

One beat   One beat

Left hind   Right hind

TROT

one beat and the right front and left rear leave the ground as a unit together creating one beat you have trot. Keep in mind the horse is using diagonally opposite feet that are working together to produce one beat. The trot has a moment of suspension, or fly time, when all four feet are off the ground. It is this fly time that creates a rough gait. Just hang around any gaited horse training barn and you will eventually hear the term, "the horse is too square." Now all this means is the colt has too much trot. When you add speed to the walk the colt will start trotting. Just like the pace, the trot is a tool we can use to develop our horse into the gait we are working towards. The trot will be discussed in more detail later in the problem-solving chapters.

For now let's just keep in mind that pace and trot are located at opposite ends of our gait scale. Both the pacing horse and the trotting horse were founding breeds for the Tennessee Walking Horse, Missouri Fox Trotter, Rocky Mountain Horse, and Racking Horse.

At gaited horse shows a horse exhibiting the pace or the trot should be penalized as having faults in their gaits. A horse that paces is too slick and a horse that trots is too square. Here I have to agree with the show world. A horse that is pacing or trotting is no fun to ride on the trail. Both ends of the scale cause problems in training the gaited horse.

I am a firm believer that most gait problems are related to speed. The horse is being ridden too fast. As a Kentucky State Trooper over the years I can honestly tell you the number one cause of wrecks in America is speed. There is no difference with the horses. Most Tennessee Walking Horses, Missouri Fox Trotters, Rocky Mountain Horses, and Racking Horses fall victim to too much speed in their early training.

Riding too fast can and will cause all sorts of training problems. Take the pace, for example, you keep adding speed to the pace more than likely you'll get a race track pace, or sometimes a gallop. You say, "Ok, I'm going to slow the colt's feet down so they don't leave the ground together on the same side." That separation or timing of the feet gives you a stepping pace. Then say to yourself, "I'm going to slow the stepping pace even slower." Now you will get what I call a swing pace. Keep in mind, each time you slow down or increase speed of the original pace you are going to get a different gait due to variations in the foot fall on the same side of the horse's body. The horse does slow down his feet, but his mind is still working with the two feet on the same side leaving the ground together.

Look at it this way, you can turn the music volume up or down with your favorite song and keep the same beat or timing. The gaited horse can add speed very quickly or very slowly to his feet to the point most riders don't feel the foot movement speed up, causing the rider not to feel a pace movement. The horse is able to stay ahead of the rider, speeding up his feet in the movement towards his desired gait. You turn the volume knob up or down the horse can change the timing ever so slightly so that it makes you late in your timing. When you do feel the pace movement you are already too late to keep the horse from pacing. Riding slowly is the best way to stay ahead of your horse. Now we have identified two more gaits associated with the pace, stepping pace, and swing pace. I will discuss this more with the problem-solving chapter: Smoothing out the gait.

The trot is much too square to ride on the trail. When you add speed to the walk you get a trot. Again, the horse can move into this gait very quickly or very slowly. The trotting colt is also able to stay ahead of the rider, waiting to shift into a diagonal gait upon the slightest request. Now some colts don't need a request, they move into a trot every chance they get. The trot presents much of the same problems as the pace when slowing the feet. You can slow the horse into a nice soft trot but the timing still lends itself to a two-beat gait. I will discuss more about the trot later in a problem solving chapter.

Each time you slow the horse's feet it is called a downward transition. Each time you add speed to the horse's feet it is called an upward transition. The very nature of the pace or trot without separation of the feet will often reveal itself when you add any speed. The main thing for now is to recognize both pace and trot are nothing more than tools for us to use to get our horses into the finished gait that applies to our particular breed. Too many owners get discouraged with the pace and trot and try to make them into a major training problem. I'm not saying the pace and trot cannot become major problems if not dealt with effectively. What I'm trying to say is, the pace and trot will present themselves whether we like it or not, so let's use both to get a finished gaited trail horse or show horse.

We can find a hint of pace and a hint of trot within the gait cycle of an ordinary walk. Use your video camera and record your horse walking on a loose rein with an even four beat gait, 1-2-3-4, select the camera speed for slow motion. When the front foot hits the ground a mere second before the hind foot diagonally opposite, feet one and three, this gives you a hint of the trot. Now when the horse's feet one and two, on the same side, leave the ground this is a hint of the pace.

Just for fun write your own.

Tasks:

Conditions:

Standards:

Chapter Eleven: The Walk - An Explanation

"There is more to life than increasing speed." Mohandas K. Gandhi

Speeding is a main cause of wrecks in the United States. In order to drop the accident rate Troopers have to run radar and enforce the speed limit laws. It stands to reason the slower drivers go the less injury and property damage. Now what does this have to do with training horses? If we will slow down the Tennessee Walking Horse, Missouri Fox Trotter, and Rocky Mountain Horse to a slow speed and give the horse time to separate his feet into a four-beat gait we'll solve many problems. The instructions in this chapter apply to the flat walk as the foundation gait for the Tennessee Walking Horse, Missouri Fox Trotter, and Rocky Mountain Horse. I believe the walk is the only teaching gait that will lead us to the finished gaits, which are the running walk, fox trot, self-carriage walk, and canter. No matter what breed you ride you should be working towards a finished gait of a high standard.

I make no bones about it, all horses have to walk off their hindquarters whether on the trail or the rail. Some of the best show horses I've trained have been trained on the trail with nothing more than a keg shoe just flat walking. I like to refer to the flat walk as the starting gait to teach and finish the horse into a proper trail or rail horse. Some industry leaders will criticize me for teaching the flat walk as foundation gait for the Tennessee Walking Horse, Missouri Fox Trotter, and Rocky Mountain Horse. I can only say to them after they have trained 200 or more horses and find a better teaching tool than the flat walk, I will listen.

Think outside the box, listen to what the horse has to say about the training and keep his point of view in mind. Between the ages of two and four is what I call the set period. During this time the colt will learn his trade within the limits of his strength. At this young age in his life he will learn quickly either good sound training or, unfortunately, bad training. During the set period between two and four years of age you must train slowly so as not to blow the horse's mind. You must have the discipline not to ask for unrealistic expectations. The colt is only going to be as good as his natural ability will allow him.

It has been my experience that you will get a hint of his natural ability during the set period. You will get a good picture of his talent around five and six years of age. The total potential of any horse is an ongoing process with years of training. Teaching and using the flat walk in the set period will ensure the colt is off to a good start.

We have to develop a standard so we know what we are trying to teach. The show world does set standards, whether you show or don't show. The show world has its ups and downs with standards that seem to change from season to season. It's very important to make the show world standards creditable with good solid training methods.

No matter how crazy some training methods are, they will work on some horses. Just use good sense when evaluating training methods. Ask yourself some ethical questions with what you're seeing as training methods. Will this training method help ensure a calm and trusting mind? Will this training method hurt my horse? Will this training method consider my safety? Would I be ashamed of how I treat my horse? Keep in mind these questions are not only for the gaited horse industry.

The Tennessee Walking Horse, Missouri Fox Trotter, Rocky Mountain Horse and Racking Horse breeds each have a set of written breed standards. Each breed industry does have other industries within the breed. I take the training very seriously to the point of asking, does my training develop the horse's mind and body for him to last well into his golden years?

Standard for trail horses:

(1) Natural head set.

(2) Over stride. (Not defining.)

(3) Head nod in the flat walk.

(4) Even four beat movement.

Developing the flat walk is an integral part of the horse's gait. You must realize from the start of training that the flat walk leaves little room for any gray areas. Any portion of a colt's flat walk that is not to standard causes a second rate performance somewhere down the road. Finding the standard horse for the flat walk is not a trip in the desert without water.

A good place to start is in your back yard. Find standard horses in your area, go and take a look at them. Don't be bashful about meeting the owners. Spend time with the owner and watch him or her ride the horses. Don't forget your list of ethical questions regarding training methods. Tell the owner you are learning about gaited horses and are interested in teaching your horse to walk. Ask as many questions as you can. Be polite and ask if you can come back to observe. Hopefully, he or she will let you ride the horse. The more you ride a horse doing the correct gait the better your chances of success are when teaching your own horse the correct gait. I highly recommend you find the standard horse that knows how to walk off his back end. When you ride a good one, you're hooked in the gaited world.

An even four-beat gait needs to be explained so there is little doubt as to what you are training as a standard. Let's re-visit gait identification again with the lesson of the small boat. Imagine four people placed in a small johnboat, two seated in the rear side by side and two seated in the front side by side. Now imagine in your mind each person represents a leg of your horse. Let's go ahead and visualize and number each person just as we did the horse's feet. The person seated at the left rear (1), the person seated at the left front (2), the person seated at the right rear (3), and the person seated at the right front (4). Our movement cycle count will start with number one.

Now persons one and two are working and paddling the left side of boat together with one stroke, lifting and paddling at the same exact time. This is the left lateral side working together to have one stroke, or one beat, just as the pacing horse does. Now jump to the right side of the boat. Person (3) and person (4) work together with one stroke lifting and paddling at the exact same time producing a second beat. You now have a pacing boat. The boat has to go straight ahead, meaning both lateral sides have to work together creating one beat at a time. Just like the horse, the boat moves forward being support laterally on both sides. The pace is a two-beat gait being supported laterally from side to side. You will feel the horse shift from side to side. There is nothing smooth about this gait. We need to break the pace up in order to get the legs working more independently of each other into a four-beat gait.

Back on the left side of the johnboat, if the person seated at the left rear (1) makes a stroke a second or two before the person seated at the left front (2) you have a stepping pace. The next progression is the person seated at the right rear (3) makes a stroke a few seconds before the person seated at the right front (4) to complete the stepping pace stride. Here is where most owners get confused or think the horse is doing the right gait.

Let's break the stepping pace down even more by delaying the timing between the oarsmen. The only way to do this is to go slower. Realize you want to separate the paddles (feet) into four equally timed strokes. Again our boat person (1) starts his movement - a good slow even stroke, completes the stroke and takes the paddle out of the water. Number (2) boat person starts a good slow even stroke, completes the stroke and takes the paddle out of the water. Number (3) person starts a good slow even stroke, completes the stroke and takes the paddle out of the water. Number (4) person starts a good slow even stroke, completes the stroke and takes the paddle out of the water. You now have slowed down the paddles (feet) into evenly timed strokes (walk). The gait is now an even four-beat gait with each leg moving the same amount of time with each step.

Teach the horse to use his body first to develop proper muscle groups to overcome many of the pacing problems commonly seen. There are no quick fixes. This will take time. The horse has to be ridden slowly to develop an evenly timed gait.

This brings us to this point of confusion. Some trainers learned that adding weight to the front or rear of the horse's feet delays and breaks up the timing, which will modify the gait. One can quickly see that the big-lick horse is doing a modified pace. The plantation and light-shod horses do a modified stepping pace.

I can honestly say every good horse I've started had the ability to step from the hindquarters forward. The thought of adding weight to the horse's feet to get a good gait without proper training is nonsense. The keg shoe will serve most trail horses faithfully. The show horse will require much of the same though.

Now some industry leaders advocate restricting the colt's hindquarters from moving forward in a natural, free stride. This camp believes it is in the best interest of the breed not to have more than 18 inches of overstride. Here is the problem with this thinking, they forgot to ask the horse about his point of view on how to use his hindquarters. I'm not advocating a big overstriding show horse on the trail but what I'm saying is each individual horse must find his natural balance. The Good Lord gives all horses the ability to walk out of the hindquarters but some have even more ability. Now that is called talent.

It should be noted, the very reason the dressage horse has to learn to go sideways (lateral work) is to get the swing we take for granted in our gaited horses going forward. The point being, don't mess with nature. Let the horse tell you what the horse needs. A high-headed horse, hollow in the back, disconnected from the hindquarters will always do a tail bobbing lick.

Headshake is the counterbalance of motion. I will go so far as to say headshake is poetry in motion. I love to watch a good head-shaking horse rolling out from his shoulders with the feet landing flat. The head shake starts in the shoulder with the head and neck lifting up and down in a timed manner. Balance is a very delicate feel that can be destroyed by too much gait modification in early training. You can get something that looks like a flat walk with action devices, weighted shoes, and other gimmicks but as soon as the gimmicks are gone the horse loses his ability to walk off his hindquarters.

The horse should nod his head with every stride. The head nod counterbalances each leg that is off the ground in flight. The horse counterbalances the hindquarters with reach and drive and the front end as each foot is lifted from the ground. To see counterbalance in the hindquarters, isolate and observe a rear foot. Watch the colt's rear foot swing or drive forward and you will see the head go down. Now as the same hind foot hits the ground and pushes back taking a step you can see the head go up. Feeling this takes time but it is nothing that an owner can't grasp in the seat of his or her pants.

You can also watch counterbalance with the front end. As each front leg is picked up the colt's head will come down and counterbalance the foot that's off the ground. Balance in the colt cannot be cheated or taken lightly. Balance must be developed with the utmost care. The old saying, "If he's not nodding his head, he's not walking," is very true for the Tennessee Walking Horse.

A Missouri Fox Trotter shakes his head through his shoulders. In the old-time fox trot lick you can see the head go up and down, left and right.

The Rocky Mountain Horse nods his head in the flat walk but goes into a self-carriage walk without headshake.

Overstride is the distance the hind foot over steps the track (print) of the front foot. That sounds simple but I find during clinics that students need time to train their eye to see overstride. The overstride is coming directly from the hindquarters with a step beyond the track left by the front foot on the same side. The overstride from the hindquarters is the step that gives you that gliding motion. Watch a horse that is doing a good overstriding step as he travels away from you. Watch his rear end swing with a nice slow back and forth motion. The tail will swing freely with each stride. When your horse is standing still or moving it will leave a track on the ground. Now the front hoof print that is on the ground will be overstepped by the rear foot on the same side as the horse moves forward.

Let's observe the overstride with the help of a friend. Stand behind a friend with both arms stretched out touching his shoulders. Now imagine you're a horse, your left leg is the horse's left rear leg (1) your friend's left leg is the horse's left front leg (2). Your right leg is the horse's right rear leg (3) and your friend's right leg is the horse's right front leg (4). Take one stride forward and stop. Remember, one stride is four equal steps. Pay attention to the next stride cycle. You will see the left shoe print on the ground. Watch for the overstride on the same side with your left foot. Your leg (1) will step in front of your friend's footprint on the ground (2). The same overstride will occur on the right lateral side. Some horses will overstride twenty inches or more.

I find the Missouri Fox Trotter a fascinating breed. This horse will cap his tracks, stepping on top of the front track with his rear foot. Some colts overstride five inches and still counterbalance their motion within a wide range of smoothness. To call this a timing phenomenon is an understatement. I can say this breed of horse is genetically programmed to counterbalance motion all the way through his body. The fox trot presents a movement cycle that still needs headshake and overstride or capping the tracks to complete a trail standard.

As with the pacing horse, the trotting horse also needs separation of his feet into a four-beat gait. This type of horse needs to add a little swing into his gait. It's interesting if you just ride the trotting horse slowly, he separates his feet into a walking gait much easier without all the timing problems the pace presents. Now it's been my experience the trotting horse's hindquarters are weak and his back is tight and stiff. This colt does take longer to develop some swing for a flat walk. Once the

From the Trail to the Rail

horse has developed strength in the hindquarters and understands how to swing his back he is set in gait.

There should be no confusion when you hear the term diagonal hind opposite. Think back to the lesson of the boat. The person seated at the left rear (1) would find his diagonal opposite seated to his immediate right rear (4). The person seated at the left front (2) would find his diagonal opposite seated to his immediate right front (3). Pay attention to timing when working with the diagonals.

Most gait definitions deal with the front foot hitting the ground a mere second before the hind diagonal opposite. Remember, a trot is the left front and right rear diagonals working together, leaving the ground at the same time, creating one beat and the right front and left rear leaving the ground together at the same time, creating one beat. The cycle is a two-beat trot.

Let's break the trot down and separate the feet into a four-beat gait. Walk the colt slowly so the front foot hits the ground a mere second before the hind diagonal opposite you now have a squared up walk. Hopefully by now you are starting to understand the art of slow.

One of the quickest ways to be successful is to understand and know when, where and how your horse's feet leave the ground and hit the ground. This comes with time and experience you'll gain with good old fashioned work.

To find a perfect definition for the flat walk regarding the Tennessee Walking Horse, Missouri Fox Trotter, and Rocky Mountain Horse is wishful thinking. I do believe the flat walk should be energetic and bold with a sense of purpose. The colt should show rhythm, relaxation, and looseness with an even four-beat gait. The horse should nod his head with counterbalance of motion starting from the rear end with an overstriding step. The overstriding step should be the natural step with respect to the gaited horse breed.

A key point to remember is that when you start forcing overstride you disturb the horse's natural balance. Just remember, the overstride should not be the defining issue.

Write your own

Tasks:

Conditions:

Standards:

Chapter Twelve: Understanding the Training Scale

"Many things will catch your eye, a few will catch your heart - pursue these." Anonymous

The Classical Training Scale is a key ingredient to successful training for any gaited horse. Years ago the German National Equestrian Federation introduced the Classical Training Scale with a set of concepts that would ensure good training.

The Classical Training Scale consists of six levels of teaching, using building blocks one step at a time. The training levels are building on a set of standards just as you would climb a ladder one step at a time. The concepts of (1) Rhythm / Relaxation, (2) Looseness, (3) Contact, (4) Impulsion, (5) Straightness, and (6) Collection, have been around for years. These concepts are time-tested and there is absolutely no reason to re-invent the wheel. The only way these six concepts will not help you is if you do not apply them.

The Training Scale gives you a place to start and assess your training system. More importantly, it will correct problems if you apply the concepts and teach one step at a time as noted. As you gain experience you can and will be able to train in all areas of the scale at one time.

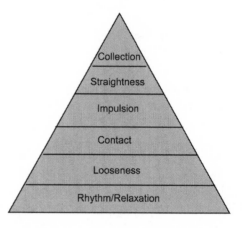

For starting the young colt it's imperative we understand levels one through three. I can say with certainty that Classical Training is the art of directing and obtaining your horse's willing obedience in the accomplishing a task. You've heard this before. It's called leadership.

Rhythm and relaxation are the first step of the scale. When I use the term rhythm I mean nothing more than gait. I can say either the horse has a nice four-beat rhythm or the horse has a nice four-beat gait. Confusion rears its ugly head when rhythm and tempo are used as the same meaning. Tempo is how fast or how quickly the horse is moving his feet. I like to see a horse move in a nice four-beat rhythm with a slow even tempo. Think of it this way, if you're dancing to a good slow four-beat song and the band keeps the tempo at an even slow speed you probably won't step on your dance partner's toes. Now if the band speeds up the tempo (still playing a four-beat rhythm) more than likely you are going to step on some toes. Finding the right tempo for the song "Home On The Range" and then changing tempo to "Let's Do The Twist" can add

From the Trail to the Rail

some real confusion when teaching a four-beat gait.

Each horse has natural rhythm. It is up to us as owners to find that rhythm. The best and only way to find natural rhythm is to work the horse's mind and body in relaxation. You can rest assured, rushing problems are relaxation problems. Relaxation is such an integral part of the horse's training it cannot be slighted in any way. You can bet when the horse gets a soft look on his face and feels soft in his rhythm, relaxation is present in his body.

Looseness and suppleness are the horse's ability to bend and follow his nose. The starter horse has no braces in his body. He can bend laterally or longitudinally without stiffness. You can see supple muscle groups working together in a loose harmonious push and pull manner. Looseness gives the right amount of swing in the hindquarters.

Not enough attention is paid to the gaited horse's back or top line. A supple back will move in harmony with a four-beat gait. Stand behind the horse and have the horse walk away. You can see the barrel swing over the supporting hind leg that's on the ground and then alternate the swing to the other side when supported by the other hind leg. You will see the swing in the gait is developed through looseness.

Contact is the amount of pressure you put in the colt's mouth. I find if you want a light front end, you need light contact. There is no doubt about it, contact is the most difficult part of equine training. Getting the right amount of contact in the horse's mouth takes a few years for the horse to learn. When starting a young colt using a mild bit is a wise choice to keep the colt from overreacting. Good contact stays away from pulling on a horse's mouth. Pulling on a colt's mouth dulls the mouth and keeps the front end on the ground. Developing contact with a light feel will lift the shoulders off the ground using the hindquarters.

Impulsion is the pushing power coming from the hindquarters, the energy coming from the hindquarters moving forward through the rider and recycling back to the hindquarters. When you feel this motion it is often referred to as the horse hitting a good gait. When the gaited horse is ridden too fast the impulsion becomes difficult to feel. The powerful feel of impulsion and tempo becomes a problem when the colt is not given enough time to develop impulsion in the walk. Keep in mind, when you slow the tempo the power of the hindquarters and natural rhythm become evident. The colt will step underneath himself, lifting and freeing his shoulders. It can take as long as two years to develop good power from the hindquarters. When gaited horses are ridden too fast they move towards a hot, hollow, stepping pace movement or a short, tense trotting action. Going fast does not have a thing to do with good impulsion.

Collection has as many definitions as there are breeds of horses. I have seen colt after colt trained into a high headed, hollow backed horse with white eyes, gaping mouth and flaring nostrils all searching for collection. My definition of collection is, "Collect the horse's mind first and let the horse collect his body." I tell students collection is a process of training, not the result of bitting rigs, tie downs, and other training gimmicks.

There seems to be a fascination with head-set training. You can go to any horse sale and watch novice people buy horses. They constantly buy horses with a high head set. Matter of fact, other than color, head set is all they see. The appeal of false collection with gaited horse has sold many fractious horses to naive owners. Keep in mind, putting a colt in a frame of collection before he is mentally and physically ready will not work. If your colt was started with a performance lick and then culled 90 days later, more than likely you've got training problems both physically and mentally. I believe less than 4% of horses survive this method. The ones that can handle the pressure and make it past three are super talented horses with a lot of heart. What happens to other 96% of horses that did not make? You got it! They are sent to the trail or plantation divisions. Skipping the first few concepts and going straight to collection develops serious, dangerous holes in the training foundation.

The modern show horse training methods have veered into using short cuts to produce a successful show horse in shorter time. Greed coupled with the flash and bang of the show world using high stepping two-year-olds to produce a colt in less than ninety days is fractious training at best. This behavior seems to be the norm across the board in all-equine industries whether you are showing horses or racing horses.

The old saying, "Make haste slowly." comes to mind. If you have a good colt, take your time and enjoy the journey. In my opinion, it's just as easy to go slow and train the colt to a high standard with years of trail and rail service. A good sound leader of horses does not skip any of the six concepts listed in this chapter. He uses the training scale to teach with building blocks one concept at a time.

Don't let anyone tell you we don't have quality trainers in the gaited world. Now more than ever you can find quality-trained horses. Find a good trainer as a role model and learn.

All new knowledge is a deeper understanding of what you already know. You are adding information on top of information one layer at a time. Building a system of teaching does require that you gain experience by hands-on training. I have started so many horses over the years I tend to lose count. I try to start at least 8 to 10 trail prospects a year to gain experience and keep my timing. I can say it is a fascinating journey. Each horse is a puzzle that requires time, love, and patience to train.

Letting a horse find his natural balance working off his rear end takes time and hard work. Most of the time, with good training it's what you don't do that will make a great horse. For example, teaching the horse to work off his hindquarters. Most heavy weighted shoes will cause the horse to labor pace. A good horse can do the trail and a show gait without any gimmicks. With proper training and time using the training scale you can produce a great horse in accordance with his talent. Give the colt a chance to use his body correctly, realizing you cannot nail on a gait. A young colt is very capable of making tracks on your face if you don't get it right. Don't blame him if you go too fast and jump some key concepts. The colt has the right to protect himself.

Living in Kentucky, I've had the opportunity to work with and observe many good gaited horse trainers. All of them will give freely of their time to teach you if you are truly interested in learning about the horse. The great thing about these master trainers is they are still seeking knowledge from the horse and play the training scale like a master violin. If you can find master trainers in your area (there are only a few) spend as much time with them as you can. These folks are roses among the thorns. When it comes to training there is no magic rope, bit, bridle, saddle or other training method, as others would lead you to believe. It all comes down to what's inside of you and your ability to develop your character. The horse is a mirror of our character. The horse gives us the ability to restrain our negative side and lets us cultivate our positive side.

The classical training scale is not only for horses. Take a look at the same classical training scale and how we can apply the concepts to owners. For the sake of brevity let's just ask six questions regarding the owner. As an owner, do I ride the colt with the right rhythm in a relaxed manner to establish consistent training? Do I keep my back loose to help the colt swing his back? Do I understand how much contact (pressure) to use in the colt's mouth? Do I understand how to use my body to obtain slow impulsion for more hindquarter power? Do I sit straight with both seat bones on the saddle? Do I collect my thoughts before I start riding?

The connection between human and horse lets both man and animal become one with each other. The horse will always be a reflection of his owner. It's amazing how quickly a horse will pick up on the owner's character or a new owner's character. Taking this classical training scale a step further, it fits task, conditions, and standards to a glove with each training area concept. I hope you're now beginning to see how leadership affects every aspect of training.

Write your own

Tasks:

Conditions:

Standards:

Chapter Thirteen: Seat, Legs, Hands

"If the rider's heart is in the right place his seat will be independent of his hands." Piero Santini

All good horsemen and horsewomen will agree with this saying, "Seat, Legs, Hands coordinated together in a smooth action assist the horse to achieve his best gait." Have you ever wondered why this saying starts with the seat first? The seat is the control center that starts all requests and fine-tunes the balance of the horse to the hindquarters. As riders it is our responsibility to ride the horse from the hindquarters forward. The seat, when used properly, will hold the horse together and assist the horse in developing a consistent gait for a smooth and gliding ride.

 When I think of the gaited seat I think of a total seat that involves your two seat bones, pubic bone, and the thighs that support a soft feel. In the old days growing up on a farm I always saw people using three leg stools to milk cows as opposed to four point legs. Why? Because the three point stools were stronger and supported weight better. Keeping your two seat bones and pubic bones deep on the saddle also forms a three point base triangle offering the same stable support. Taken a step further, it can make all the difference in the world with safety when you ride your trail horse. You do not have to be an Olympic rider competing for a gold medal to get the benefits of a stable seat. Remember, a good seat is a lasting impression on your horse's back. Your horse knows if you care about his back, and by the way, that's where his gait is located. More on that later.

Let's take a closer look at the seat, legs, and hands and how all three affect you and your horse. How do we achieve a good seat? Start by getting your two seat bones deep into the saddle. Sit in the saddle like you see a jockey sitting on his horse. This position puts your two seat bones deep in the saddle. When taking a break on your horse's back, this is a great position to rest your horse's back.

Now you want to drop your legs onto the horse's side and let them fall around the horse's sides like you would lay a lead rope across his back. Now here is the key, line up your pubic bone, belly button, and sternum, in a straight line to your shoulder or collarbone. You actually rotate your pubic bone up and forward to come in line with your stomach and chest. When this alignment lines up it will form a 'T' when intersecting with your shoulders. You now should be sitting on your seat bones, not your pants pockets, in a good stand-up seat. You will also feel your pubic bone touching the saddle. Fill in the rest of the seat with your thighs letting your heels go slightly downward. In this new seat just take deep breaths into your stomach or belly breathe. This will release your back for great trail rides. This position may feel awkward at first so give yourself time to develop this concept. Looking at this seat from the side you see ear, shoulder, hip and ankle forming a plumb line. Using this rider alignment, if the horse should suddenly disappear you have a good chance of landing on your feet.

An up side down horse. Notice the hollow back, tense neck and high head. The mental attitude is with the flight responses activated. The sway in the back is causing the hindquarters to trail out. The dip behind the withers is a pit fall to good, balanced riding.

Now look here. The top line is round. The horse is working through his back. The mental attitude of the horse has changed. He is starting to relax. Work from free walk to a flat foot walk.

Take this concept a step further, when you sit lined up just behind the withers it gives you an opportunity to influence the horse's balance. When a horse speeds up and hollows out in the top line, more times than not, you will feel your feet go forward because you are not matching his strength with the feel of the seat. For example, when your horse goes forward quickly without notice you suddenly feel your shoulders and head go backwards while your feet go forward. You are now a full stride behind the motion of the horse and most of the time he is in control of the situation. Some horses, love them or not, will take full advantage in evading you with this situation. Most of the time it becomes a game with the horse asking you questions to see if you know the answers.

Keep in mind there are some camps that advocate riding pleasure horses with you seat rolled back onto your pant pockets. This type of riding can and will get you into trouble, depending on the horse's personality. Over time the hot, tense horse will get hotter when ridden with this mutated seat. Remember, your seat plays a big role in the horse's attitude and the way he moves. Why? Because where you sit on the horse's back is the first and most critical area of communication with your horse, not the bit as most people think. It comes down to how you use your seat regarding the first line of communication.

Now we add insult to injury when we forget about the driving seat with our feet on the dashboard and start pulling on the horse's mouth. You have just created the upside down horse. Sadly, some riders and even professional trainers blame this on the horse for having behavior problems. No matter how you spin it, a mutated seat is a mutated seat.

Even great riders lose their seat every now and then but regain it back very quickly without notice. If your goal is quality long distance trail riding and exhibiting show horses you must understand the concept of classical riding. The best way to achieve this seat is to open your legs, feel the contact with the seat bones, public bones and thigh muscles, then close your legs just enough they lie gently against the horse. This spot I'm referring to is just behind the withers.

Stay walking and working slowly in a good lined up seat. Notice when you add speed or the horse adds speed you feel yourself falling out of position. Just work on getting back into position by opening your legs like bird wings off the side of the horse and feel for a deep contact with your seat. Then set your seat again in the correct position. When your seat falls out of position and when you struggle to get back into a good lined up seat you are learning to sit the horse. Always remind yourself, don't ask more from your horse than your own seat can handle. You are learning to hold the horse together with the seat.

Try this exercise, walk five strides check and evaluate your seat. Open your legs off the side of the horse, get lined up, close your legs and sit deep following the horse's motion. Now this will do many things to smooth out the gaited horse. If you are riding a hot and tense horse that wants to become high headed, hollow backed and upside this riding seat will teach him to calm and stay round. Over time, this seat concept will absolutely work wonders in getting a hot, tense horse to develop a round top line and a smoother gait. A good seat gives you the opportunity to have independent legs and hands.

Several years ago, while trail riding in Hoosier National Forest with my cousin Susie, we walked around a sharp bend on the trail. Susie's mare saw a deer and ejected Susie straight into the air with one power-ful buck. As she was being ejected from the saddle Susie rotated 180 degrees in mid-air to come to rest landing on her feet facing the mare. Susie was still holding the reins the same as she was riding. This had a profound effect on me, but to see the look on her face was priceless.

When you are developing a good working gaited seat you become in-dependent of your hands and legs. Keep in mind we are not abandoning our hands and legs. What I mean by an independent seat is the ability to use your and hands and legs independent of your seat. Find your bal-ance without pulling on the horse's mouth. This seat gives you the first connection with the horse's back. I will go so far as to say the control center for coordinating all your movements starts with your seat and then with the horse. Most owners think connection starts with the reins to the mouth, for example to turn, back up, change gaits, stop etc. I call this forehand bridle riding. A coordinated system of aids that starts with the seat and is controlled by the seat will open doors to lighter front ends on the trail and higher front ends on the rail.

A trail horse most of all needs to walk off his hindquarters. To get your horse on the hindquarters the horse has to shift his balance to the rear. In simple terms the withers are higher than the croup when the horse is moving. For the trail horse this is noticeable, but not to the extreme you see in some horse shows. What I'm referring to as an independent seat will allow you to feel this shift in balance. If you're not thinking about your seat you will completely miss the shift in balance. When the balance shifts and the colt is walking off the hindquarters, this is referred to as hitting a good lick.

Remember, when you ride with your legs stuck out in front of you like you're sitting in a recliner chair or like when you are a passenger in a pickup truck putting your feet on the dashboard, you are behind the motion of the horse. When in this position, your seat bones are driving into the horse's back. This will result in a high headed horse with a hollow back doing a tail bobbing lick, meaning the hindquarters are disconnected, and the horse is cut in two. In this mutated seat position the rider is usually leaning backwards and the pubic bone is off the saddle. This seat position produces a stepping pace, a rack, or a hard pacing action. You can say this is an independent place of the leg in the wrong position.

Keep your legs softly around the horse's side and bring your toe directly under your knee. This will bring your feet under your center of balance. There should be even weight on both seat bones. When you glance down you should not see your toes.

When you sit on your pubic bone and lean forward and off your seat bones this is a perched position. You are now putting your horse on the forehand. What happens is the horse never truly comes through from the rear hindquarters. He becomes very heavy in hand. This heaviness requires you to support your horse constantly. This mutated seat will develop a fifth "leg," your hands, to support your horse's movement. You attempt to hold the horse's head up with the bridle reins causing your hands to become very busy. The over active hands add even more problems for the trail horse.

Now the hands can also take on an independent role, good or bad, depending on how you use them. Every now and then you hear someone say he's got good hands. What this person is referring two is soft hands that don't create problems. You will see a good rider time after time holding the reins with just enough weight to keep the reins from flopping. The quickest way to get a dull mouth is by pulling on both reins at the same time. In order to have soft hands you must have a stable seat. The hands must also be independent from the legs. A good rule to remember with the hands is, "Don't ride with the brakes on." If you get one thing out of this book remember my little my poem, "Light hands produce a light mouth causing a light front end, starting with the rear end." Much more on this later.

All of this talk about seat, legs, and hands seems to be overkill for the weekend trail riders. You may ask yourself, is it worth learning to ride from the rear forward? The answer is absolutely, yes. When you line up your pubic bone, belly button, sternum, and collarbone to form a 'T' with your shoulders you are freeing up the horse's top line. You are now letting the power come across the back from the hindquarters to the horse's mouth into your hands. Your legs are underneath you with a soft feel on the horse's sides. All of this action serves to recycle forward energy and balance the horse's motion, no matter how tough or extreme the trail footing. Using a good lined up balanced seat and riding slowly, you can develop a great flat walk no matter what breed of gaited horse you ride.

Following the horse's walk with your seat bones will develop into deeper areas of understanding that will open many doors in your riding. I've worked with many students who will never come close to reaching their full potential because of seat or lack of seat. It all comes down to this, are you willing to develop your leadership skills in the art of riding? Riding is not easy, it takes work and dedication to achieve a level of mastery that requires for you to walk the valley. Books, videos, TV stars and other publications can only assist. You have to walk the journey yourself.

The more I teach students and the longer I work with students the more I'm convinced we need to get it right the first time. Working at Mid-West Trail Ride in Norman, Indiana, has truly been an eye opening experience. During a ten-year period I've had the pleasure of serving as the gaited horse clinician. During all major holiday periods there are approximately three hundred trail riders and horses. To say you see every imaginable horse and rider combination is an understatement. I've had the opportunity to work with novice riders and seasoned campaigners. I always welcome the challenge to work with riders and horses. Nowhere in the world could I gain such valuable experience and find great friends over the years. Teaching owners is very rewarding experience. You see certain riders reach a level of horsemanship that is the envy of any show world.

Now I add this here because 99% of the problems I see with horses start with the owners. The question I always ask myself is, "Why do certain people make good riders and others struggle with the same old problems no matter how many times they change horses?" No matter how much time you spend with certain riders one-on-one, it's the same old-same-old. They seem to struggle along spinning their wheels in a wet cornfield.

Time after time during a weeklong ride I work with the novice riders (age does not play a factor). The next year I see tremendous improvement. The following year I see total connection. I'm always fascinated about this connection and what led to this improvement. The answer always comes back the same. The leadership principle of know yourself and seek self-improvement is the number one result of my findings. These owners spend time with their horses. Most students report a total time in the saddle is around 1,200 hours a year for a three-year period. These riders are special. They have passion and desire to learn like most people want air. I must admit that to watch students with this type of desire and motivation become excellent with their horses is invaluable experience.

To understand the seat, legs, and hands requires a good look at co-ordinating the aids. I like to think outside the box and say separate the aids first, then teach coordinating the aids. This may be a better teaching system. If you think about what we are trying accomplish. Just this one aspect alone will require a lifetime of learning. Each learning step is a new and exciting learning of deeper knowledge. We just keep building and building on top of what we already know.

When I see a good rider I think of self-seeking reflex actions. What I mean by this is the rider stays ahead of his horse and applies the needed seat, leg, hand as a reflex action, as determined by the situation. He has the experience to make the right decision with reflex action without conscious thought. You see this all the time in your daily life. For example, after you have been typing on your computer for a few years you just type what you think with little regard to the steps (fingers) involved. When you first started typing you had to break things down in small steps, one at a time. Same thing when starting a young colt, break down the training into small steps. Eventually you get to point where you realize that a self-seeking reflex action is experience following experience.

Write your own

Tasks:

Conditions:

Standards:

Chapter Fourteen: Developing Contact

"Yielding to pressure is important, regardless what you are doing with a horse." Joe Walter

When we think of contact with the gaited horse we have to explore much further into the horse's mouth and look at different concepts and terms that shape our trail horse's needs. One area of confusion is having so many different ways to describe the term "contact with the bit." Make no mistake about it, this is the most difficult task of communication to obtain with your horse. Just for fun, ask five good riders what the term, "contact with the bit," means to them and I'll bet you get five different answers.

Now let's take this a step further. We live in what is known as the "Information Age." To help us communicate with each other we use telephones, radios, televisions, cell phones, pagers, e-mails, and satellite communications systems. Even with all this technology, we still can't talk to each other without dropped calls and other human confusions.

Add all this up with so many different bitting methods and the pressure of trying to communicate with your horse can become overwhelming and difficult. The good news is bitting the young horse does not have be a mountain to climb without ropes. To develop contact, we must define contact as a total package of seat-leg-hands, taken one step at a time, slowly. Granted, you must have a stable seat, meaning a seat that allows you independent balance from your hands and legs. For this reason it's best we start with a snaffle bit that offers tongue relief and then progress to the shank bit. A snaffle bit that offers tongue relief is more forgiving with the young colt and he will tolerate this training process more easily. Never forget seat, legs, hands coordinated together produces total soft contact.

If you don't have an independent seat, please seek professional help before you start developing contact under saddle. Let me say it this way, the seat, legs, and hands are all independent actions of each other requiring support from each other at different times. An example would be, using Western cues, to turn a young horse to the right put weight on the right seat bone and right stirrup, open the right leg just like a gate. Use the left leg to push the shoulder to the right then finish with elastic hand only the amount of pressure considered necessary. All three actions are independent movements that lead to contact. Although most owners will tell you contact starts in the mouth, if you are not using other aids you can develop a bridle horse that is very heavy on the front end.

Turning to the right, using English riding cues, would be to advance your right seat bone forward, use a soft inside leg, bring your outside leg back, use a direct inside rein, and support the turn and bend with the outside rein.

Remember there are two primary ways to use your cues, the Western discipline and the English discipline. I start any colt with Western cues and develop into an English system as he gets older, no matter if he is going to the trail or rail. In both disciplines the final goal is for the horse to move forward or laterally with a stable seat, off the leg, with a soft hand contact.

Keep in mind that in bridle riding the number one problem is with horses staying on the forehand. The hands are connected to your seat and the bit in the horse's mouth. If your hands are overly active it will cause you to miss the timing with your horse.

I've met a lot of old time trail trainers who are great at getting the right bit in a horse's mouth. Most of them will tell you it takes a certain amount of bit pressure to square up a horse (the weight of a strawberry in each hand). The comment most often heard is when you get the right amount of pressure in the horse's mouth he falls into gait. Now this is a little misleading in that you're not told that the horse has had countless hours of flat walking on a loose rein, building the top line into gait, to get him ready to accept contact. Some horses do require just enough pressure to keep the reins from flopping. With any more pressure than that you can get a good racking horse.

The gaited horse brings a headshake to the table. As we know all horses nod their heads to a certain degree in an ordinary walk. When we separate the feet into a flat walk we have to consider the right amount of contact to assist the horse in shaking his head. The head shake is what we want. When I first starting riding gaited horses I heard over and over again from the old master gaited horse trainers, "Don't ride your horse outside his head shake." When I thought I was getting it right I would hear, "Slow your hands, you're getting the horse out of time."

Constant pulling on the reins and overactive hands will diminish head shake to a head peck. Soft hands, giving fingers, elastic wrists and stretching elbows will assist in developing head nod, which is the counterbalance motion needed in the flat walk. Hold the hands soft and let the horse work on the bit, and not the bit work on the horse.

Some horses develop a deep head shake and will drop their head down, bump the bit and raise the head back up in good rhythm. Some gaited horses require more pressure in the mouth than others. It's a very individual thing but no horse needs jerking in the mouth. Hold the bit softly with just enough feel to keep the reins from flopping.

During start up training and re-training I only use two rein effects, a leading rein (open) and a direct rein. The leading rein leads the horse into the turn. An example of an open rein, for a right turn, hold the right rein in your right hand, extend your hand and right arm out away from the horse's body to lead into the turn. Open your left hand to support and regulate the horse's shoulder and bend of the neck. Use a strong left

From the Trail to the Rail   63

leg to push the horse right to assist the right turn.

For a direct rein keep the hands active at the withers with squeezes and releases. You also want active legs to help complete the turn. To turn to the right with a direct rein squeeze the right rein with the right hand at the withers. Bend the horse around the soft inside (right) leg. Use your outside (left) leg back behind the girth. The left hand controls the amount of bend.

Look inside your horse's mouth. You will see potential pressure points: the tongue, the lower jaw, the bars, and the roof of his mouth. Now the real point I'm trying to make is if you look closely you will find his heart and soul is located where you are going to hang a piece of metal.

Always keep this in mind you can have the best equipment: Bits, saddles, bridles, books, and training theories known to mankind but without understanding correct contact, you don't have much. Many people buy a horse that is gaiting great when purchased, and then wonder what happens a few weeks later to their horse's gait. More than likely it's a contact problem. Too much contact with a shank bit usually leads to rearing, head tossing, refusing to turn (most of the time to the right), high head, hollow back, rushing, and the list goes on and on. With too little contact, the horse flops around on the forehand like a fish out of water and does not developing his engine, the hindquarters. The old saying, "The only bit that works on a horse is a bit of knowledge." is as true today as it was 100 years ago. We could spend days or weeks on this subject.

For an entry level starting point let's look at just three basic concepts of developing contact: Hold, Release, and Reward.

Rocky Mountain Horses, Kentucky Mountain Horses, Tennessee Walking Horses, Missouri Fox Trotters, and Racking Horses are different breeds, but they all have one thing in common. Each individual horse must be taught a complete understanding of the release of pressure as a reward. When you take a young child for a walk with no traffic around, as long as he is safe you don't hold his hand, you release his hand and let him play. If he starts doing something you don't like, or you come to a busy street, you again will take hold of the child's hand. This is the same concept with your young horse. When the horse is doing well, or what you want, release the hold for a reward.

I use the term "hold" because that's what using a bit is all about, "holding," not "pulling." When you put the bit in the horse's mouth the desired effect is for the horse to act upon the bit, not the bit upon the horse. Just look around on the trails or horse shows you will see rider after rider forcing the bit to act upon the horse.

I firmly believe the gaited horse needs tongue relief to gait properly. A snaffle bit is a non-leverage bit that has no curb/leverage action. A snaffle is jointed in the middle and has many variations of rings: D-ring, egg butt, and other combinations. When used correctly this bit sends one signal at a time, exerting less pressure on the tongue, bars, lips and corners of the mouth. A mild snaffle bit signal gives us an opportunity to put pressure in the horse's mouth without causing an overreaction, especially with the young horse. Why? Because it doesn't restrict the horse's tongue. The key is to keep the horse calm and not give him a reason to overreact. As a general rule the thicker the mouthpiece the milder the bit, and the thinner the mouthpiece the more severe the bit.

Place your snaffle bit and bridle on the horse without reins. Now for the first few times, don't have the bit pulled up into the corners of the horse's mouth, creating wrinkles, just a nice fit almost to the corners of the mouth. We want the horse to lift and hold the bit himself. If you start with the bit creating wrinkles in the horse's mouth you have already established no-release contact.

Let the horse wear the bit around in the corral getting used to lifting and mouthing the bit. Ten to twenty minute sessions for a few days are fine. Just stick around so if he gets into trouble you're there to help. After three or four sessions the horse will stop mouthing and will accept the bit. When the horse learns to hold the bit I have no problems in lifting the bit just enough to place a wrinkle in the corner of horse's mouth.

Now add your reins to the snaffle bit and stand beside him. Pick up the left rein in your left hand, hold and squeeze. You are now putting pressure on the horse's tongue, lips, and left corner of his mouth. Hold this pressure until the horse gives by moving his nose and eye to the left, then immediately release the pressure for the reward.

Step to the right side of the horse, pick up the right rein in your right hand, hold and squeeze. You are now putting pressure on the horse's tongue, lips, and right corner of his mouth. Hold this pressure until the horse gives by moving his nose and eye to the right, then instantly release this pressure for the reward. The amount of weight or pressure you put on the reins is like holding two baby birds, adding only a small amount more pressure if needed. It's important that you maintain the hold and give only when the horse gives first.

How long should you practice this concept? This training is progressive in nature and will need to be presented to the horse with the same applications at different stages of development, such as using the shank bit, which works off the bars of the mouth. I'll have more on that later. The key is to take your time and train slowly to build a good foundation in the horse's mouth so he understands that the bit is associated with a reward for giving the right response. Developing the reward into lightness will open many doors of performance.

Lightness is the one area that gets the rear hindquarters driving and the front end reaching. You hear people say you have to able to take a hold of a horse to help him. There is truth in this statement but more times than not riders try to pull the front end off the ground. Keep working towards lightness and never dull the mouth. You have probably already guessed. You are teaching Classical Conditioning. When you get this right, the sky is the limit.

I do not use lateral flexion exercises, bringing the horse's nose around to the stirrup, on a colt just starting his training. There is no need for this type of heavy-handed training for a young horse. If you take the front end away from the colt and drop him on the ground, you can create more problems with the colt escaping through the shoulder than you can solve later. For an older horse that needs some correction and domination this type of training may be somewhat effective.

Reading the horse's mouth requires a working knowledge of resistance. A lot of horses will go through some conflict with the bit, especially when they are not comfortable. Most horses will tell you about this matter through resistance. Recognizing the signs of conflict in the horse's mouth will save you training time, mouthing problems and your pride when the horse has had enough. Never do anything that will violate trust in the horse's mouth. When a horse has his tongue hanging from the side of his mouth, or is tossing and ducking his head in all directions, the horse is not happy in the mouth. Now in all fairness to most new owners, this behavior came with the horse when they purchased their horse. It still comes down to this, he is your horse now and a reflection of you, so guess who is responsible to train or re-train the horse?

You say, "I'll just send the colt to good bit trainer and get him re-trained." This is a noble idea but you still need to understand contact yourself because you are the owner and primary trail rider. I have not met a trainer who was hired so the owner could ride double behind him. The point I'm trying to make is a good trainer cannot give you his hands. You have to learn it yourself with hard work and desire.

When you start a young horse there will most certainly be times when you need to correct the colt, especially on the first trail ride. If you use a ten-inch shank bit to disengage the hindquarters you're not correcting anything. You will get an overreaction from the pain in the horse's mouth. Just a few overreactions can and will lead to all sorts of behavioral problems. I see this time and time again with horses showing signs of resistance on the trail or rail. Good contact calms the horse's mind, which solves more than half of the training problems.

I have the opportunity to work with many problem horses. I can honestly say contact is the number one problem leading to dysfunctional behavior on the trail. I cannot begin to tell you how many times working with owners and horses at clinics I have removed a long shank bit from a horse's mouth. The horse cannot relax and does not have a calm enough mind to meet the rider's unrealistic expectations. For example, if you are trying to get good contact for a light front end the more you pull with a long shank bit the more your horse raises his head and hollows his back, staying completely grounded.

Now there is big percentage of horses, usually older, whose minds will calm quickly when there is no bit pain. When you get a calm mind you have a good starting point to train or re-train your horse.

Contact is different for every individual horse you start or own. As owners and riders we have to strive for light contact. I am more than ever convinced gaited horses need training in classical lightness in the mouth. Total contact requires you to train your horse, which takes time and patience.

Review

Tasks: You, as the rider, develop an independent seat and learn to coordinate your seat, legs, and hands for light, total contact to achieve the horse's best performance. Adjust your performance expectations so you can appreciate the horse's natural abilities.

Conditions: Ride the horse using only the most basic equipment: a simple snaffle bit and a saddle. Use nothing more than plain keg shoes, only if needed to protect the horse's hooves from wearing down too much. Self-discipline, concentration, and practice, practice, practice to develop your own balance and coordinate the timing of your cues.

Standards: Maintain an independent, balanced seat at all times. Hold, release, and reward the horse with light contact, training your horse with time and patience.

Chapter Fifteen: Teaching the Flat Walk

"In your handling, seek a balance between firm and gentle." Charlene Strickland

If you can say there are 29 different ways to get to Rome then there are 29 different ways to train a horse. Some of today's methods I don't particularly agree with. I find most methods are too quick in pursuit of a fast buck. I like to start young horses just like you would put a picture puzzle together. Each piece of the puzzle has to fit together one piece at a time to see the colt's personality and talent. The average time for me to train a colt is about two years. Granted, the colts are turned back out after 90 days for some soak time but nonetheless it still takes me two years with most colts and then you are only at a respectable place to start. Now some horses are God sent colts, which are much easier and quicker to train.

Somebody is going to have to take the time to ride the young horses in order to develop a good training foundation. We would not think of sending young police officers out into the world without proper training. Would you let your doctor operate on you without proper training?

Teaching the colt to flat walk is a gratifying experience. Each colt is different and will require different needs at different times. My training method, which I call the "Art of Slow," has two simple rules to remember. Rule number 1 is: Take your time and ride slowly. Rule number 2 is: When things go wrong refer to Rule number 1.

Prior to starting the initial training phase take some time and write out your tasks, conditions, and standards for your personal training system. Don't forget to include the classical training scale.

All horses do a regular walk regardless of breed. When you just walk your gaited colt on a loose rein with no contact most experienced owners will call this regular walk movement a dog walk, free walk, trail walk, or ordinary walk. When doing a dog walk you are not concerned with a headset. The horse is relaxed and allowed complete freedom to stretch out and down with his head and neck. Using a snaffle bit keep very soft contact in the mouth and watch the reins swing back and forth. From the ground you see this same type of swing with the tail like a pendulum back and forth.

Many gaited horses can perform both pace and trot but are likely to prefer one or the other. It's important to observe which gaits your horse has a tendency to do when under saddle. Most gaited horses trot on the lunge line so it's difficult to get a good feel of their tendencies unless they're under saddle. Our goal is to develop a good flat walk using the gait the colt is inclined to perform.

Ride on a loose rein for a month just to evaluate the colt's individual preference. During this evaluation period don't worry about shoeing or gait modification, just go forward finding a comfortable movement in a relaxed manner. Developing the dog walk is the first two requirements of the training scale (1) rhythm / relaxation and (2) looseness.

From the dog walk we can start establishing upward and downward transitions. The dog walk (free walk) must be carved in stone in the colt's mind. The dog walk starts the process of separating the feet into a four-beat gait. Some trainers call the dog walk the "dreaded camel walk," with good reason, because some big overstriding colts separate the feet into four corners that feel like a hump on each step. This is what we want. As you ride, try to feel the motion in the seat of your pants. Get a feel of the colt's neck stretched out and towards the ground. You should see and feel a strong balancing up and down headshake.

Now all of this so far is great if we were in a perfect world, but more colts than not will give you a high head and hollow back. It's worth repeating, the higher the horse's head the less brains and the lower the horse's head the more brains. Getting the horse's head stretched out and down is part of training that is missed too often even with seasoned trainers.

The tack required is a snaffle bit, a saddle, and a riding crop. You will be starting on the ground, so wear boots and a helmet, and use other safety equipment. Always remember the horse does out-weigh you and can hurt you. Consider his point of view, he is a prey animal and has built-in reflexes to protect himself. Your safety always comes first.

Your horse needs to be sacked out (desensitized) with the riding crop all over his body, until he learns a relaxed total acceptance of the riding crop. You will begin this exercise by standing on the ground close to the shoulder of your horse. Use your riding crop and start rubbing the crop all over the horse's body. The goal is to de-sensitize the horse, so you don't get an overreaction when you tap the horse to go forward.

After the horse is sacked out so he accepts the riding crop, stand on the left side of your horse's head and use your left hand on the left rein to gently lift the bit up and down in the horse's mouth. Vibrate with your fingers or use a very gentle shaking motion. Look for a response that the horse is moving his tongue up and down under the bit and starting to chew. This response indicates the horse is relaxing the poll behind the ears. Now, move the horse's head two to four inches to the left 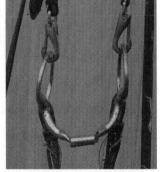 toward you. Use your riding crop in your right hand to gently touch the horse's hindquarters. When the horse takes a step with the left hind leg pay attention to the elevation of his head. When he starts to drop his head, release and follow his head down with the rein.

This training is progressive in nature and will require some time to teach. Remember with the gaited horse, as the hind leg drives forward the head goes down. The stretch down of the neck and head comes from the release.

You should be aware that some horses will be reluctant to drop their head. This is because of stiffness and tension, braces, in the poll, neck, and top line. With this kind of horse there is definitely built-in tension. Most horses are taught man-made braces with poor training. However, some colts are born high-strung which leads to built-in braces.

What I call "braces" in horses are muscle groups that will not stretch and relax. With this type of horse you can teach dropping and stretching

the head at the halt on the ground. Tack the horse in a halter and lead rope. Then stand facing the horse. Hold your left and right hands on the lead rope under the halter. You can, at the halt, put downward pressure on both reins and ask for lowering or stretching of the head down. As soon as you feel the horse's head go down just a little bit release the hold. Reward the horse and repeat. Don't try to pull the head down, the horse will just stay tense and brace against the pressure. With patience and practice, releasing every time the horse lowers his head a little bit, the horse will learn to drop his head and stretch more. This exercise develops a long-term relaxation program for a better trail horse.

Remember, the stretch down comes from the release. Just stay at this until you can move your right hand behind the poll with light downward pressure, add downward pressure to the lead rope with the left hand, and

From the Trail to the Rail

feel the horse stretch into the release. With some high-tension horses your arms may get tired but you will feel what I'm talking about when the stretch is released. For safety reasons, pay attention to where your head is when the horse drops his head below his withers and stay out of the strike zone. He can raise his head very quickly without warning. This exercise should be done on the ground. How long will it take to teach this exercise? It can take from one hour to a month, depending on the tension in your horse.

The key to understanding the benefit with this exercise is long-term relaxation. I am not saying you have to go around rolling peanuts on the ground. Your goal is to find the natural position for your horse's head carriage. When I think of the ideal head position for the horse to carry his head on the trail I think of the 1968 Ford Mustang vehicle that has the horse emblem on the grill. If you can recall this grill ornament, the horse's head is just out from the neck about even with the withers.

Getting the horse to drop his head down can be easier under saddle with some horses. Ride the horse in a small ten-meter circle. Use your left hand as the leading rein and apply just enough pressure to feel the rein in the horse's mouth. When the inside leg is engaging release your fingers on the left hand and follow the head down. Just keep repeating the  pattern until the horse's head is below his withers. I recommend teaching this on both sides of the mouth to help establish a calm-down cue.

Just like your truck or car you have controls to manage forward energy, gas, and brakes. The more controls you have to manage the horse's forward energy the safer it is for you and the horse. A calm and trusting mind will always be the best control.

During this period of dog walking the one-rein stop can be introduced to the horse without difficulty. Pick up the inside rein. Disengage the rear end with the left rear leg crossing over the right rear leg. As soon as the horse steps over and stops moving his feet release the inside rein. The one-rein stop is an old control method designed for a snaffle bit. It's important to remember when using a shank bit that you need to wind the horse down into a small circle, slowing the speed down prior to disengaging the rear end. Using a one-rein stop with a shank bit at speed can roll a horse over on his side. Just take a look at the old Western movies and watch how the stunt riders rolled the horses over on their sides. You're not immune from rolling your horse. The key with a shank bit is to slow the horse down into a small circle with no speed first, then gently apply the one-rein stop.

Using a snaffle bit, walk your horse down the side of the barn about four feet from the wall with your left leg next to the barn wall. Ride the horse slowly. Pick up the left rein and turn the horse into the wall. The left hind leg will roll over the right hind leg. Let the horse stop and think about the movement. Keep in mind if you do this too fast the horse will crow hop with his hindquarters and not get a good cross over, meaning not a good stop. There can be no doubt in your mind, the one-rein stop requires 100% trained to standard.

Still working with the dog walk (free walk), let's add an additional movement to the one-rein stop. Again walk the horse slowly beside the barn wall with your left leg beside the wall. As before, pick up the left rein, turn the horse into the wall, roll the left hind over the right hind then stop. Next, pick up the left rein, bring the front end across to your left and continue dog walking to the right. You will feel a heavy front end when you bring the front end across. This is natural for the horse to be on the forehand. The more you practice this the lighter the front end becomes. The rear-end-under and front-end-across does for the gaited horses what shoulder-in does for dressage horses.

In the dog walk get the colt to follow his nose turning and stop-ping. Stay with the dog walk until the horse is established in (1) rhythm relaxation and (2) looseness. Just as with people, the horse has to be able to relax. Using the dog walk gives us a place to go back to when things go wrong. When the horse gets upset or tense we can always go back to a dog walk on a free rein to find a calm mind. For example, we are working the horse in the flat walk and the horse becomes spooked and up goes his head. You can feel the tension under saddle and he is not going to settle. You know that without (1) rhythm and relaxation and (2) looseness the horse will just stay tense. You have to have an area to go to find (1) rhythm and relaxation and (2) looseness. Roll the rear end under, drop the horse back into a dog walk and establish a calm mind.

During the Gulf War my company operated out of a base camp. The base camp was a secure place where the troops could get some rest and feel better about things. When we went back out with convoys it did not take long for tension to creep back. We always looked forward to going back to the base camp. What this has to do with horses is, the horse will always look for R and R, meaning rhythm and relaxation. The horse can work out of the base camp (dog walk) into other gaits then back to base camp (dog walk).

When you add speed to the horse's gait you add a good dose of difficulty. We have to teach the colt to separate his feet by adding speed and regulate the amount of difficulty by keeping the colt's mind calm. The method of going into gait and back to dog walk is called transition (meaning a change). Getting the dog walk carved in stone is no gray area of a base camp of operations. The dog walk (free walk) will be a part of the horse's complete career.

The transition from a dog walk into a flat walk is not a big deal. Don't feel like you are eating dinner with your hands tied behind your back. Many people would lead you to think gaiting a horse is difficult, but it's not when you use the horse's natural ability. If the dog walk is not established you're not ready to proceed. If the horse is spoiled with a high head and hollow back you are not ready. You will be amazed how common sense training will set you and the colt up for success.

Up to this point the horse more than likely will not need any shoes, but pay attention to the wear of his feet. At any time shoeing is needed, a good quality keg shoe will fit the bill.

Remember this formula: Square = slow timing of separated feet.

Start working the horse on the ground, just playing with separating the front end from the rear end. Remember you are dealing with a young horse so it's not about wearing him out on the ground or under saddle. The horse needs go back to the stall with the same liveliness of feet as he went to the crossties. Don't forget you are training both mind and body.

Play with the horse on the ground for about twenty minutes with rest time. Pay attention to the walk on the ground. Make sure your lead rope snap is not hitting the horse under his chin, aggravating him and causing him to toss his head. Look for evenness of gait, headshake, and overstride. Lunge both ways and look at each side of the horse. Try getting a feel for how the feet are moving just up out of the dog walk. If the horse starts trotting or pacing on the lunge pay attention to what he does when he slows (downward transition), look for the evenness of gait, headshake, and overstride.

Now ask yourself a million dollar question. What is going to happen to this horse when I add weight to his back? While still playing on the ground look very closely at the back. Keep in mind a majority of horses will trot on the lunge and yes, you have some that will pace. It's been my experience that the horses that will pace on a circle have weak backs. Always remember there are no absolutes with horses. If you say it's this way every time just stick around and one will come along that will prove you wrong. I get tickled at clinicians who get paid to tell what a colt can do by measuring conformation. Save your money and go to a fortune-teller. It will be about the same statistical outcome.

In the flat walk the back is level. In a good flat walk you will not see a dip or a bow in the back. If you look real close you can see the horse's barrel right at the top line kind of swell up with a little pride. Here's where we get into trouble with the gaited horse. When we add weight to back we must have a strengthening period to develop the horse's back. The young horse's back will not be able to sustain gait without proper conditioning. In a nutshell, take the time it takes to develop each colt's individual top line with the correct muscle groups working together with a drive from the rear and reach from the front.

A nice lady sent me an e-mail and said her trainer told her that her young horse could be ridden with a high head set because he would get stronger with age, it would not hurt her horse. Now that is like telling an owner you can jump out of an airplane without a parachute; you will land softer the longer you fall. What happens with this type of thinking is the wrong set of muscle groups are developed and then the horse has to be re-trained.

You just opened a new can of worms with top line development. The time spent at the dog walk at the start will help develop a good top line.

Prior to riding, you need some experience of what the flat walk feels like under saddle. Find a good standard horse. Check with the owner and ask if you can take a few rides. A good horse will shake his head, over stride the front track, and the gait is even. The horse will come together but is still relaxed. You will feel a strong sense of going forward with a smooth flowing rhythm. You can feel the beat as the front foot hits the ground a mere second before the hind diagonal opposite leg. The lick is bold, the hindquarters drive forward with no high wasted hock action, the front end reaches forward with the feet landing flat. A good true flat walk will always have two or three feet flat on the ground. The even rhythm of the flat walk is always four separated feet. Each step takes the same amount of time as the step before it. Keep the gait slow and steady at about the same cadence as walking up a steady slope. Move up the hill with purpose but don't overdo it.

After a twenty minute session of lunging, tack the horse with a snaffle bit and saddle. Ride for few minutes at the dog walk to get the horse relaxed. Now for the flat walk, ask for a hint of speed, just a notch above the dog walk. Squeeze with both legs. As soon as the horse starts to speed up close both your hands to hold and catch the energy. You should feel a more pronounced drive from the rear and an increase headshake but the four beats remain even, not tense or quick. Ride several strides, drop the contact and let the horse go back into the dog walk. It's important to keep the flat walk pure in its rhythm. The rhythm is relaxed with looseness. There is no place for tension. If tension and stiffness are added into the mix the horse will begin to pace or trot and you set yourself up for more work down the road. Don't get confused with looseness in the flat walk. You're letting muscle groups work together with push and pull with tone of strength, not tension.

Build an upward transition (change) into the flat walk for several strides, then drop contact for the dog walk. When you squeeze your legs and feel the horse respond forward, catch the energy with only enough hand pressure to feel the horse's mouth. Don't try to pull or set the head at this time. Head set will result from the driving action of the hindquarters.

When the rider's legs stimulate the hindquarters for more impulsion followed with the right amount of hold from hands, then the rider gives an immediate release into gait as a reward you are building a solid foundation in training. As a result, the horse will adjust his head set with the proper natural elevation. I think outside the box here, I only want the horse to move his nose approximately two inches toward his neck for a headset. I want the horse to learn to stretch forward into the bit, not jam the head and neck into the withers. Pulling on the horse's face will not only put you on the forehand but will keep you on the forehand. Keep this in mind when the mouth is dull and lift is gone.

Getting the horse in front of the leg is when you squeeze there is an immediate response with the horse going forward. When you squeeze and don't get a go-forward response use a riding crop behind the leg. Practice with the crop for several strides, then ask without the crop. If you get a prompt reaction praise the horse and keep him in front of your leg. All you want is a complete go-forward attitude with light leg squeezes. Keep in mind, you are not coming out of a starting gate. Keep the ugly word speed out of the formula. Square = Slow timing of separated feet with impulsion. Speed has nothing to do with impulsion. Remember impulsion is the carrying power of the hindquarters. As an important note both speed and a severe bit at this stage of training will teach tension. The old saying, "An ounce of prevention is worth a pound of cure." sure applies to training young horses.

The stable seat lets the legs squeeze first and the hands hold and re-

THE GAITED HALF HALT

SQUEEZE WITH LEGS
COUNT:
ONE THOUSAND ONE

CATCH ENERGY WITH HANDS
COUNT:
ONE THOUSAND TWO

RELEASE/SOFTEN INTO GAIT
COUNT:
ONE THOUSAND THREE
FINISHED

Length of half halt about three to four seconds

PURPOSE:
SHIFTS BALANCE TO THE HINDQUARTERS
TO LIGHTEN THE FRONTEND.
(REBALANCES THE HORSE)

From the Trail to the Rail

lease into gait. You've probably already guessed you are practicing a half halt. The half halt action of your body should not take over three seconds to complete. Count the action in your mind: Thousand one, squeeze with your legs; thousand two, catch and hold with your hands; thousand three, release softly into gait.

Work the horse on straight lines beside the barn wall. Keep his nose in front and in the middle of his chest. The half halt action is not simultaneous with one action, there is a pause between the legs, hands, and the release. The release is the reward. Make sure you release your legs to rest lightly on the horse's sides. Get in touch with your horse's mouth to try and determine how much release it takes. Some horses require a complete soft release and others a soft partial release. It's very important that you send your horse forward with the legs (driving aids) before you use your hands. Why? Using your hands first is like driving your car with your foot on the brake pedal.

A word of caution: In a young horse the driving action of the half halt can be dangerous if you don't read your horse's personality correctly. If by nature the horse is hot, nervous, flighty and tense, use only the appropriate amount of half halt (driving aids) as needed to keep the horse from blowing a fuse. By design some horses are sensitive and others are laid back. Feel out each individual horse and use only the appropriate amount of seat, legs, hands so as not to create a 1,000-pound rocket. With a young horse I would never recommend squeezing with the legs and holding with the hands at the same time. Just use some sense when teaching the half halt. The bottom line is you want an action from the horse not a reaction.

Building the transition from the dog walk (free walk) into the flat walk will develop a horse that will walk off his hindquarters. After applying the half halt you can feel his barrel swell up with pride. He will almost burst out of his hide with an attitude of "Look at me!" With a good horse you can feel the shoulders roll forward with arching reach. What you are feeling are the horse's shoulders filling up with energy staying in front of your legs. It will take training time to get this feel (experience). It sure is worth the effort. The main things to remember are to keep the colt relaxed and keep speed out of the formula.

A good flat walk keeps the gait even in time. A good, consistent flat walk doesn't allow an upward transition that drifts towards other variations of mixing and matching gaits. When the horse is stepping forward he is landing flat on his feet. When sets his foot down there is no rolling motion, just a flat-footed walk. Try to feel the timing of the feet. Don't let the horse move his feet faster, make him stay slow in time with your seat.

Review

Tasks: Teach the horse to lower his head and stretch out and down to

From the Trail to the Rail

develop a calm-down cue. Teach the horse a one-rein stop with either rein. Practice relaxation and rhythm and looseness at the dog walk. Begin developing the flat walk a few strides at a time using half halts and releasing into gait.

Conditions: Begin teaching the head-lowering exercise with a halter and lead rope working in your small pen. When riding use a snaffle bit to develop the calm-down under saddle, teach the one-rein stop and practice the dog walk and flat walk.

Standards: The horse should lower his head and stretch into the bit when the reins are loose. One-rein stops must be 100% on both reins, resulting in a complete stop every time. The dog walk must be perfectly even four-beats on a loose rein maintaining relaxation and rhythm at all times. The flat walk adds impulsion while maintaining the same flat-footed movement, perfectly even four-beat timing, relaxation and rhythm without tension or drifting into mixing and matching other gaits. The dog walk and flat walk must be 100% to standard.

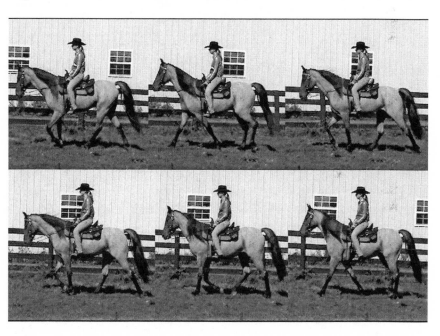

Chapter Sixteen: Developing the Gear Box in the Flat Walk

"To find new things take the path you took yesterday." John Bourroughs

Using a series of exercises coupled with beginning half halts will start the young horse well on his way for great trail rides. Many readers may think all of this is too much for a trail horse. Let me remind you, all horses no matter what the job or discipline, must walk off the hindquarters. The horse, by nature, walks off the hindquarters and is very efficient at liberty, but when you add the weight of a rider to his back the weight becomes difficult. The horse has to be taught balance with a rider on his back.

Building a gearbox with the art of slow requires patience to let the process grow. The horse should be walked slowly to give him time to separate his feet in his mind. Set yourself a goal of working the horse slowly with self-discipline. Now what I mean with self-discipline is, believe in what you are doing. Realize it takes time with the art of slow to get the horse consistently walking off his hindquarters. The bottom line is, if you don't believe in yourself the horse will find you out and know you're not serious about your training.

The exercises in this chapter are described with upward transitions into the flat walk and downward transitions back into the dog walk or free walk. The upward and downward movements are key transitions for all future training. For example, when you drop contact from the flat walk the colt's head goes down to find relaxation. Keep in mind good sound temperament in breeding stallions and mares seems to be getting lost in the gene pool at this time. As owners we have to compensate and teach for a good mind.

The circle has to come into training sooner or later. Getting the horse to walk a good circle starts with a basic understanding of the circle. The circle will always be present with groundwork or mounted work with the horse. When you are on the lunge line you've got a circle. Riding in the show ring when you ride from a straight line then into a curve you've got a half circle. When you ride along the rail in a sixty-foot round pen you've got a circle. When you ride in the woods you make many small circles around trees. The list can go on and on. When you ride a circle you can ride counterclockwise the first way of the ring or clockwise the second way of the ring.

Keep this concept simple. When you are standing in the center of a circle and the colt is moving to the left around you, you are watching the horse's left side on the inside of the circle. The outside of the horse would be the right side. Now reverse direction of travel. Standing in the middle of the circle and the horse is traveling to the right you're watching the horse's right side as the inside. The horse's left side is now the outside. Regardless of the direction of travel the inside will always be the side you're watching.

Riding good circles requires a bend to keep the horse following the curve of the circle. Believe it or not, it's the bend that helps get the horse straight. When riding the horse straight beside the rail the horse should be following the track straight. Stand behind the horse and watch him travel away from you. If you only see two hind legs moving away from you the colt is nice and straight following the tracks of the front feet. When the horse is moving straight the hind legs are blocking your vision from seeing the front legs, this is what you want. If you see four legs moving away with no influence from the rider your horse is crooked. What happens when the horse's hind feet don't follow the front feet into the curve is he is not bending his body in the line of the curve so he cannot walk the curve straight. Don't fall out of your chair. Even a curve has to be walked straight.

Often a rider can create a crooked horse. This idea of flexing a horse's head to the left and right to touch your knees for some kind of magical control will cause a crooked horse. The colt will try to please you by bending his neck too much every time you ask for either rein contact, then he will learn to escape through the outside shoulder.

If the rider is sitting crooked on the horse, with more weight on one seat bone than the other, the rider displaces and offsets the feet so the horse cannot track straight. A good balanced seat with equal weight on each side will go a long way in helping the horse to track straight.

Tack the horse with a snaffle bit and saddle. Ride the horse at a dog walk on a free rein for a ten-minute warm up period, getting him to relax and settle in his mind.

Ride at a dog walk in a twenty-meter circle. Feel the horse separate his feet, feel the overstride, and look for the headshake. I first teach the circle with gaited horses walking into a curve from a straight line. The inside barn aisle or a fence corner will do just fine. Make sure the demands of the curve are not too difficult (too small) for a young horse. The ideal curve is an oval track with twenty-meter curves at each end.

Ride the horse on the straight line going into the corner. Ask for the half halt by squeezing with your legs. As you feel the energy go forward catch and hold with your hands, then release into gait. Keep the rhythm slow and steady with a sense of purpose. Follow the bend of the curve by turning your neck with the horse's neck as you look between your horse's ears along the curved line you want the colt to follow. As you start looking into the curve bring your inside seat bone a hint forward. This action will add weight to your inside seat bone. Bring your outside leg back to regulate the hindquarters from swinging out.

How far you bring the outside leg back depends on the curve you're riding. In a big loop bring the leg back only two or three inches. The smaller the curve the further back your outside leg needs to go to hold the hindquarters. Use the left rein to lead the colt into the turn, vibrate the inside of the rein just until the horse flexes enough you can see the inside nostril or eye. Use your left leg softly at the girth for the horse to bend around and to assist the left rein. The right rein is supporting. It does not allow the neck to over bend to the inside.

When you get to the center, or apex, of the turn and start coming out of the curve using the same aids as riding the curve and give the horse-another half halt. With most horses you're going to feel a balance shift to the rear with a more pronounced headshake and more square in gait, especially if your horse's tendency is to pace. As your horse comes out of the curve and walks into the straight stretch you may feel him drop back onto the forehand. This is ok. The horse is not strong enough to carry you in gait. As a matter of fact, go ahead and reward the colt for doing a good flat walk, let the rest be long in the work and dog walk down the straight stretch.

There are many different ways to use the half halt. Here are a few: Use a half halt going into the curve and a half halt coming out of the curve. Use a half halt only for coming out of the curve. Use a half halt only when going into the curve. Feel how the inside hind leg steps up to the outside foreleg. Recall part of the definition of a flat walk is when the front foot hits the ground a mere second before the hind diagonal opposite.

Coordinating the aids will become a reflex action with time. Working into a curve is the quickest way I know of for getting your seat, legs, and hands coordinated together as riding cues. When riding into the curve I like to advance my inside seat bone only a hint forward which puts some weight on the inside seat bone. This action brings the outside leg back. Now after you advance the seat bone don't freeze the seat bones still, follow the horse's back motion with your seat. Your inside leg asks the horse to bend around your inside leg. The inside open rein, direct rein, leads the horse around the curve. The outside leg behind the girth limits the amount of bend by keeping the hindquarters from swinging out and helps bend the horse around the inside leg. The outside rein limits the amount of bend. All this sounds technical but it's not.

When you ride the curve for about sixty days it becomes second nature and will stay with you for a lifetime of refinement into higher levels of riding. With a more advanced horse isolate one or two areas at a time, just ride and develop your personal cues. In no time your cues become refined motor skills that require little thought. The conscious thought becomes your subconscious reflex action.

The circle is a great tool to get the horse to square into a flat walk. You ride a twenty-meter circle with the same coordinated cues as riding a curve. The only thing different is you are adding two curves together to form a circle. Words of caution, don't overdo small circles with a young horse. You will place too much demand on the joints that are not fully developed.

Don't think just because you are riding simple circles things can't go wrong. If you are riding to the left the first way of the ring and the horse does not want to bend in the rib cage use you left leg more actively. Make sure you can see the left eye in the curve, use your left leg and pretend you are pushing the leg through to the outside. Some horses will swing their hindquarters out towards the rail. If yours does this use your outside leg strongly to bend the horse back into following the tracks of his front feet. Think of a train going into a curve to the left. All wheels on the left side and right side of the train will stay on the track. If the outside wheels of a train start coming off the track, bouncing up and down, you can expect a train wreck. If the horse is not following the curve but has his nose looking to the outside of the curve, flex him to the inside so you can just see his inside nose and eye.

Instant impulsion is what I call hill work. The quickest way for you to feel the flat walk is to work the horse up a moderate hill. I'm not talking about a hill so steep you have to hold on to the horse's tail to get to the top. I'm talking about a good steady incline that requires an effort from the horse. The hill sets the horse in a position for strong driving impulsion from the hindquarters. Now don't confuse impulsion with speed. What you're feeling is impulsion, not speed. This is the same feel you want when you are flat walking on level ground. When the horse moves up the hill he is in a position that requires and makes him use his hindquarters. Dog walk the horse a few times up and down the hill feeling the feet separating.

At the bottom of the hill give the horse a half halt and let him step into the flat walk. Ride the flat walk slowly to top of the hill and drop contact back into a dog walk. If your horse likes to pace make sure he walks slowly back down the hill. At the bottom of the hill stop and rest, let the horse soak for a few minutes and think about what you are trying to teach. Give a half halt and ride again back to the top of the hill. Look between your horse's ears and feel for the flat walk. This time when you get to the top of the hill don't stop, keep walking on level ground. Pay particular attention on the level ground when the colt drops onto his forehand. When you feel the horse is not using his hindquarters you've lost the impulsion.

Two thoughts come into play. First is your ability to recognize when a horse is working off the hindquarters. The second is you're dealing with a young horse so he will not have the strength at this time to carry you into gait. He will give you hints of good things to come.

In your mind and seat you must know and recognize what impulsion feels like. The hill exercise will teach you the feel of impulsion quicker than any other exercise. Actively riding your horse forward for this feel of impulsion is what you're trying to accomplish. Speed has no place in finding impulsion. It takes time for you to build muscle memory in your mind and the seat of your pants. Go back and forth with hill work for your own experience in identifying and understanding when the horse is using himself from the rear forward. When you get to top of the hill on level ground see how far the colt can walk without losing impulsion. More importantly, how many strides did he go before you identified that he fell onto the forehand?

The carrying power of a horse depends on getting your colt into shape. Keep in mind he is just a baby and needs time to mature. Getting him legged up and developing the top line is why I work so much with the dog walk. Most young horses are started at around two years old. It stands to reason the colt needs time to develop into a mature horse.

When you ride the colt to the crest of the hill pay attention to his breathing. Don't over work the horse into labored breathing, let the rests be long in the work. Work in the dog walk for relaxation of the horse's mind. Let the horse have plenty of time to stretch into the bit with his head below his withers. This is the time in the horse's training to develop the right muscle groups with easy, slow training. The transitions between the dog walk (free walk) and flat walk will amaze you on what you can accomplish with your horse. My training method teaches tasks, conditions, and standards using the old classical training guidance. The old masters had it right long before modern man.

Using ground poles on the ground is a great way to develop your flat walk gearbox. A gearbox on your tractor or truck allows you to add speed in whichever gear you select. The gear selected in the gearbox will not break into a faster gear. To better understand this, drive your car in low gear and notice that you can add variations in speed without the vehicle changing into faster gears. What the gearbox brings to the table for the trail horse is the opportunity to develop his natural gait by adding speed to the walk without shifting into a pace or trot.

With non-gaited horses you can cruise with an automatic transmission. Just add speed from the walk and you'll get a trot. With the gaited horse we want an automatic transmission that ranges from a dog walk to a flat walk by adding speed slowly, giving the horse time to separate his feet. Teaching your horse to walk out fast, believe it or not, is done

From the Trail to the Rail

slowly. It should be noted that all horses do an ordinary walk so no matter what gaited horse you choose to ride you can develop a good flat walk that makes a great trail horse.

To get started, tack your colt with a snaffle bit and saddle. With the art of slow in mind, letting the horse do an ordinary dog walk (free walk) is the first priority. Let the horse dog walk on a loose rein, no contact, just a relaxed, easy, four steps going forward. He will, in time, learn to drop his head and stretch out to the bit.

If his head remains high and his back hollow this is where we use the cavalletti (ground poles) to help achieve relaxation and start dog walking. Place four ground poles (cavalletti) 8 or 10 feet long on the ground approximately 8 feet apart. You can use boots for protection on the colt if you desire.

Take a few minutes to lead the horse over the ground poles from the ground to get him used to the footing. Now, under saddle, start the horse walking over the first cavalletto. You will probably find some hesitance. Just keep urging the horse forward in a free walk and on a loose rein. It's been my experience that after the second attempt the horse will start walking on his own account and will need little coaching from you. Look for the horse to drop his head and feel for his back to rise. When he lowers his head and raises his back you are now separating his feet in the art of slow. Now don't despair, you will not create high hock action. Just keep working with the horse and feeling the horse separate his feet. Use this pattern two or three times a week. Gradually build up to about 15 or 20-minute session. In a couple of weeks you will have the dog walking muscle memory carved in stone.

When you make the last step over the last ground pole and have completely cleared the last ground pole, give the horse a half halt, squeeze

From the Trail to the Rail   83

with your legs, catch the energy with your hands, and release the fingers into gait. Ride a notch faster than the dog walk. You're now on your way to flat walking. You will feel the impulsion just as in the hill work. Riding slowly in the dog walk over the ground poles into the flat walk is a good transition for developing a great gearbox for fun trail riding.

Some trainers are shy of ground poles thinking they will teach a two-beat gait such as a trot. When using ground poles as described in this chapter you have to ride slowly, not fast, in order to separate the feet into the walk. Get the feet separated in the colt's mind. Keep the ground poles about 8 feet apart. The important aspect is you are developing the right muscle groups for the top line. Making upward transitions coming off the ground poles using a half halt into gait and then downward transitions into the dog walk or free walk is just good sense training.

Riding in tall weeds or straw stacked about ten inches high is a good exercise to get the colt square. Prior to riding in any high weeds make sure the footing is safe. If you can't see the ground where your colt is stepping, get off and check the area. Always check to make sure there are no potholes, old fence wires, or postholes. Ride the horse in a dog walk to let him stretch down and forward just for some relaxation. Get the feet separated into a four-beat gait with a good dog walk headshake. Let the horse step into the weeds and see if you feel the flat walk without a half halt. Most horses will step into a good flat walk. If you get this, just go with the motion just as if you gave a half halt. Find the contact and stay in time with the colt's mouth. Drop the contact back to a free walk when you clear the weed patch.

Just for fun, ride beside the weed patch in a dog walk. You want clear footing riding parallel about two feet from weeds. Give the horse a half halt. Feel if his balance shifts onto the hindquarters. If not, step the horse into the weeds and feel if he shifts onto the hindquarters. Make sure you praise the horse for doing the right movement when he starts hitting the right beat. Get the feel of this in the seat of your pants.

Food for thought: What's happening in the weeds can and does become confusing. Most owners think the horse is lifting his forehand higher because he has to step over the weeds. Now this is true, he does have to step higher to clear the weeds. So armed with this knowledge comes the idea of gait modification using the front end with weighted shoes, actions devices, shackles, and other training methods. The problem is owners are training the colt from the front end to the rear end. Just as soon as the colt clears the weeds or the action device is gone he falls back onto the forehand.

The lift we need to clear the weed patch has to start from the hindquarters. The colt has to be taught to use his hindquarters first in order to lighten the front end. Powerful steps from the rear allow him to lighten his front end and roll his shoulders in a reaching arc forward.

This is very easy to see from the ground. Have someone else ride your horse and observe the movement. I am more than ever convinced using the half halt with time in accordance with the colt's strength and talent will teach the colt to walk off his hindquarters.

Ride what I call the letter 'J' turn. Picture the letter 'J' in your mind. Think outside the box. For fun, use your lawn mower to mow out the letter 'J' in the field. I use my lawn mower to cut out 'J' patterns, circles, and serpentines. Cut the pattern out big enough for easy walking. I don't recommend doing this to your neighbor's hay field. I also recommend you check with your spouse before attempting this in the front yard. If you don't want to use the lawn mower, baking flour works great to print out the letter 'J', circles, and serpentines. Your goal, using the 'J'-pattern, is to feel the inside leg to outside rein, when the front foot hits the ground a mere second before the hind diagonal opposite.

Dog walk to warm up the horse. Feel for relaxation for a few minutes. Then ride the horse straight down the line of the letter 'J'. When you start into the curve of the 'J', half halt and feel for the colt to square. Hold a little more pressure on the outside rein. You will only get two or three strides of a square lick. The more strides the better. Keep in mind it takes a lot of strength for the horse to carry a rider in gait. The deep engagement of the inside hind leg causes the horse to square up and drive to the outside rein. When you hear someone say the horse is "deep" they are referring to the horse stepping deep from the hindquarters.

Every exercise in this chapter is teaching the horse to use his hindquarters first and foremost. Getting the colt's hindquarters set under saddle is the first area of concern in riding. I have watched time after time the special trail riders who do nothing more than walk their horses into gaits worthy of a king. All they do is stay on the trail hour after hour on a loose rein riding transitions from a dog walk into a flat walk. Riding the horse with simple transitions develops the mind and muscle tone without tension. Use downward transitions back into a calm base camp.

Try to keep tension from creeping into muscle memory. There will always be a balancing act between a calm mind and tension. A good, calm minded horse is much easier to train than a colt that blows a fuse every five strides. Take your time and try each exercise slowly to find the one that is right for your horse. When you find the square flat walk stay with that feel for as long as it takes, going back and forth between dog walk and flat walk with upward and downward transitions. The average horse takes me about two years to bring out his full potential. Take the time it takes to get a good slow dog walk into a flat walk. A top horse comes to gait very quickly. You just have to stay out of the way and let him develop slowly but you run the risk of losing the horse if you train too fast. Many top prospect horses are lost between the ages of two and three years. In later chapters I'll discuss more options you can use in solving gaiting problems.

Review

Tasks: Teach the colt to travel straight on a curve. Teach the colt to make a correct 20 meter circle. Develop a range of speeds within the flat-foot walk. Strengthen the colt's hindquarters and teach him to walk off his hindquarters.

Conditions: Continue riding the colt in a snaffle bit, keeping a calm mind. You may start working in a pen or along on oval track. When the colt is ready progress to riding in a pasture then go out on the trails. Ride the colt slowly up hills. If the colt persists in pacing ride slowly over ground poles in the pen gradually working up to 15 minute sessions several times a week; Use 'J' turns to encourage the colt to step deeper under himself with the inside hind leg; Ride the colt slowly over plowed ground or weeds.

Standards: The horse always travels with his hind feet following the tracks of his front feet with head, neck, and body aligned to match the direction of travel on straight lines, curves, and circles. The horse maintains even timing and a calm mind while using a range of speeds within the flat-foot walk and lifts the forehand by increasing the impulsion from the hindquarters without tension or hurrying.

Chapter Seventeen: The Top Line

"Every time you ride, you're teaching or un-teaching your horse." Gordon Wright

Establishing and maintaining balance is the key to finding the great gait we want and expect with our horses. Let no one kid you, this area of training is the valley we all have to walk along. Some owners make it through with very little problems. Other owners are still stubbing along but making progress in understanding. What I'm referring to is the position of the back and the relationship it has to the desired gait you want to teach. The top line is much more than a place for you to sit. Believe it or not the top line (back) is the first line of communication with the horse. The horse's back is the control center for the seat, legs, and hands. Stiffness and tension must be avoided at all costs.

One question comes to mind when developing the top line: At what age do I start training my colts? I can tell you the procedure I use and it has worked wonders for me. Every situation is different and requires some thought on how to proceed in keeping with sound training methods. I start the two-year-olds with 90 days of training, then turn the horse back into the field until he is three years old. I start back lightly at three with groundwork, fifteen to twenty minutes, and limited riding for about fifteen to twenty minutes. I work the horse up to forty minutes every other day. I like to work the horse on the ground teaching the horse to walk on the lounge and then ride twenty minutes on a loose rein getting the horse to follow his nose, turn, and stop.

During this training period (set period) I'm very concerned with where the horse carries his head in the snaffle bit. There is no place here for a high-headed horse. I get the head stretched out and down. During this time the colt is on the forehand, which is expected. I found the hard part in training a young horse is knowing how much is enough and when it's time to quit. Each horse is a different road map that has to be read slowly.

At four years of age, I introduce them to the trails with flat walking, looking for the foundation gaits. During the trail period I evaluate the colt's natural ability and potential. I like to have a minimum of ten trail rides, four or five rides with a calm horse and four or five rides alone. After this period I start riding with groups but am very selective about which group. I try to avoid the hell-bent-for-leather trail riders in order not to let my horse feed on the group's energy. You can solve many problems keeping the young horse focused and listening to you. He has no business knowing he can feed off negative energy within a group of horses. Keep in mind, that's exactly what most will do without good sound leadership from the rider.

Some camps advocate that a gaited horse will automatically start gaiting when they mature at around four or five years of age. Just ride the horse in the set period until they mature. The idea is if the gaited horse has enough strength to carry a rider he will start gaiting automatically at a later age. The problem is the horse is a creature of habit. He goes the way you ride him. When he is programmed in the top line for a hollow back at a young age he will not change at any age until he has properly developed in the top line. Automatic gaiting may be true with some horses that have not been started until four of five years of age with good genetics. The concept is a good sales pitch. But when you start riding a horse at a young age and teach him to amble because his back is too weak he will not change into his foundation gait at any magic age.

Keep in mind, the set period, the first two years, between two and four years old, should be centered on calm work. This sets up future development of a calm pleasure horse. In no way should the set period be cheated with shotgun training methods. A wise owner during this time will concentrate on getting the colt to develop harmony with his owner. The set period is the time to get mental relaxation and looseness, to develop the top line, to increase the muscle fitness with slow steady training.

This time period gives a lot of thought to the colt's mental situation. Try to determine how much is enough without blowing a fuse. Keep in mind, nothing fabulous has to be achieved during the set period. This is the time to teach the colt to work with his muscles in the top line in a relaxed condition, not in a short crimpy state. As stated before, tension and stiffness will creep into the affairs of the top line if not judiciously watched. When the horse's neck is stretched out and down, as in picking grass, this serves to lift the back and release the back at the proper level to find our gaits. Just as important, getting the back too round with a gaited horse can also cause problems. I'm not advocating you go around with the horse's nose stuck on the ground, just a head set out from the withers to help build a top line.

When you see a horse traveling with a high head, back hollow, ribcage hanging down, his necks retracts up and away from contact, and his hindquarters are disengaged. This is a hollow-backed horse which creates problems in the long run with over all training. The horse is a creature of habit and will go into this position because of habit or poor training. Every time you put pressure on him before he is ready, especially in the area of overbitting, you've got a hollow-backed horse. To say again, stiffness and tension must be avoided at all costs.

This problem is not new to the equine world. Every discipline gets a good dose of top line development problems. In a nutshell, a rider who is riding with his back hollow will cause the horse to hollow his back. You must always take this mirror effect into account. The horse will always mirror the rider's back. There are strong reflective parallels between the rider's back and the horse's top line.

Try to look at my point of view this way. A horse is made up of pain, fear, excitability, and muscle tone. These four areas encompass all aspects of horses and their training. Nature has endowed the horse with the right of self-preservation. The horse will use pain, fear, excitability, and his muscle tone to protect himself from predators, and also from you and the way you ride him. With this in mind, we have to work within the laws of nature to teach and train.

Nature has left us one area we can use to teach and solve problems with the horse. I put my own spin on it and call this area "muscle tone development." For example, when you release pressure off the bit, you release pressure off the tongue muscle. This reward is for doing the right response. You do the same thing when using your legs on the side of the horse to ask for a half halt, then release into gait. The seat bones can act neutral, or drive into the back, or tilt forward. You can use the colt's muscle strength against himself to defeat himself. A good example, would be hobbling, which is very effective training when done right.

The top line requires proper muscle tone development to enable the horse to carry you without hollowing his back. Getting the muscle tone on the top line without stiffness and tension requires the horse to be ridden with the head just out from the withers. Walking on a loose rein with the head and neck stretched out and down will lift the back and start the muscle development needed for a good horse to work in upper level positions. The position with the neck stretched out and down must become a part of the horse's life style.

I like working gaited horses in the dog walk with upward transitions then downward transitions with the head and neck stretched down and out. I don't know who coined the saying, "show the horse to the ground first", but this is absolutely the right statement for training gaited horses. If you're training show horses you will have to bring the head up eventually when the top line can support self-carriage.

Try this exercise. Take a ten-inch long piece of string, hold one end of the string in each hand, then pull your hands apart and tighten the string. Now let your hands come together about two inches notice the sag (dip) in the string. This is the same thing as a hollow-backed horse. A key point to remember is some horse don't have to have this much sag. A sixteenth of an inch with some horses will give you a hollow back.

This position can lead to many pacing problems that will eventually have to be solved with proper top line development.

Take a riding crop, hold it out in front of you with a hand on each end. Imagine the crop is the horse's back. Now bend the riding crop ends down, putting an upward bow in the crop (top line). Imagine a sunfish with the top line features of an arched back. This is the position of a trotting horse's top line. You can find the fox trot with a slightly rounded back. The running walk and the self-carriage position are at level top lines. Most gaited horse will follow along with these top line concepts. Just like conformation, one or two will come along and prove you

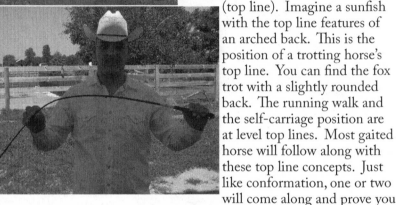

wrong. I have seen hollow-backed horses do some pretty amazing high school walking in a keg shoe but that is not the norm.

There are many different spins or names you can put on the top line, hollow back (concaved), and a rounded back (convex). There are some trainers who are of the opinion conformation will determine how the horse is going to gait. You need to understand conformation is not the sole contributing factor to any gait. So before you starting worrying about length of back, hock lengths, and angles of shoulders, please pay more attention to good conformation of mind. Then later on research your horse's body conformation. It has some merits and is worth devoting some time to, especially in breeding.

One of the reasons this book advocates a dog walk (ordinary walk) and a flat walk is to develop the top line. I've lost track of the number of horses that I've trained and re-trained for owners to take the horse home and dog walk for a year or so just building the top line into a finished gait. It is unbelievable what you can accomplish with just time and slow dog walking. Don't get wrapped around the axle with speed. It all comes down to balance, getting the horse to walk off his hindquarters with contained impulsion not speed.

Getting the horse to shift his weight to the rear requires that you have a balanced seat to help the horse, not to hinder the horse. The problem with most owners is they do not want to ride the colt slowly to build for a finished ride. On the average it takes me two years to teach a young

From the Trail to the Rail

horse to walk off his hindquarters. It is most certainly worth your time to get the hindquarters activated with the proper muscle groups pushing and pulling, working together. When the horse shifts his balance to the rear and the front-end floats, it feels like a swimming motion. I am more than ever convinced that the horse has to be dog walked into gait. When speed is introduced too quickly either by horse's personality or the rider, it will destroy balance.

Horse's normal balance in carrying his weight in the field

40% 60%

hindquarters Front-end on the fore hand

We need to teach the horse to carry his weight with a rider, using the hindquarters for 60% with a light front-end of 40%, as seen with a stallion meeting a mare.

60% 40%

Following the motion of the horse is what novices riders are told. This is a great teaching point. When starting your riding career finding the motion of the horse is one of the main ingredients of success. There are riders, less than five percent, who do this naturally without conscious thought. As you grow and become more aware of balance and how it affects your horse you soon realize you want the horse to follow the motion of your seat. When you get to this point you are no longer a novice.

When training my young horses I always start following their natural motion in the dog walk then into the flat walk. As the horse's training continues I start getting the horse off my legs with half halts. I try to just let it happen in a sense not to force anything. It won't be long before the horse will start following my seat, legs, and hands. The hands are only used to finish the movement if needed and move like molasses on a cold day.

Ask yourself some questions. Using your seat, can you feel the horse's hips dropping down? Can you feel the horse's belly move from side to side, just feeling with your seat and legs? With these two questions you can open up a new world of understanding with the word feel (experience). Take your time and think about feel (experience) with just some plain old common sense thinking. Old cowboys have been doing common sense thinking about feel with horse for years.

As the horse's left hip dips and his leg is swinging (stepping) forward your seat bone dips on the same side. Now on the same side, when the horse pushes back off the ground your seat bone will rise. This happens in alternating movement with the other side. Try to remember the leg motion this way. When the left rear leg is moving forward your left seat bone dips. When the left rear leg sets down on the ground and drives back (pushes off) your left seat bone will lift forward. Think of the wheel on an old steam engine train and how the wheel rises and falls. This is very easy to feel in a big striding dog walk. When you ride a trotting horse your seat bones move like pedaling your bike backwards. On a

From the Trail to the Rail   91

gaited horse you get the feel of seat bones moving more like a long conveyer belt. This really makes for a comfortable ride.

To help you really feel more, place your left thumb in your left rear pocket and follow the motion for a few strides. Then reverse and place your right thumb in your right rear pocket and follow for a few strides. Now this comes to mind, the good Lord in His wisdom gave us ability to separate our seat into halves, following the motion on each alternating side of the horse. If you want a higher front end for the show world you must understand these concepts to train naturally.

You can also feel the horse's barrel shift from side to side in the walk. Pay attention to your legs as the horse's barrel swings to the right and that side of his back rises. The other side, his left hind leg is stepping forward. You guessed it, your left hip then dips and then rises as the horse's left hind foot hits the ground then pushes off (drives back). Brief touches of the calf muscle against the horse's side ask for more engagement.

Using timed half halts in a curve can get a gaited horse deep on the back end. Bringing your leg farther back you can ask for lateral movement with the hindquarters. Squeezing the barrel with your legs can ask the horse to round his back. I try to use my calves to squeeze and lift the horse's back, especially with pacing horses. I am a firm believer in the half halt with all gaited horses to develop the top line for better gait and for the long-term soundness of the horse.

Keep in mind, these leg aids must be timed with the horse's leg in the right position. It's impossible to influence a leg that is grounded and carrying weight. A leg aid that is timed correctly is when the hind leg is getting ready to push off the ground and can be easily influenced with your leg aid. For a greater stride, catch the leg just as the hind leg is coming off the ground, just a touch with your calf muscle on the same side. Not enough attention is paid to the timing of the feet with your leg aids.

Riding without using leg aids will do very little in developing the top line. The term "dead to the leg" means the leg aid does not mean anything to the horse. Keep this in the back of your mind when training the horse. Your legs have to mean something to the horse's feet with proper timing of the feet. Once you understand the feet and how they move it will open many new and exciting rides with your horse. The set period between the ages of two and four coupled with good training gives us an opportunity to develop a good, balanced top line.

When training the young horse you are constantly balancing the movement to the rear in order to get the horse to use his hindquarters. When you follow the motion of horse's top line using your seat in a relaxed manner it's much easier for the horse to learn his job. A rider who is tight and tense, even though he looks like he is in the right position, will reflect this tension to the colt's top line. Another thing that happens is tension limits your ability to recognize when the colt shifts his balance to the hindquarters.

One of the exercises I like to do at clinics is to lead the horse while the rider closes her eyes and holds one arm over her head. This exercise releases the rider's back and allows the rider to follow the motion of the horse's back with good accuracy in the seat. While I'm leading the student I always ask what she is feeling. The reply is, "I can feel my seat bones moving with the horse." Or, "I feel my back moving with the horse." I try to make a point to the student that this is what you're missing in your riding with both eyes open using both hands on the reins. Your seat has to be separated into two halves to follow the alternating top line motion. Most students have a locked back and follow the alternating motion of horse in a locked pelvis position, which adds tension and stiffness into the top line.

When the top line is properly developed, you can get the horse working off the hindquarters much easier. Just remember, with a young horse take the time it takes to develop the top line. The slower you go in the long run may be the only fast way to train your horse. A keynote is that your top line has to be developed to move in synchronized motion with the horse. Give yourself time to develop your seat as a following seat.

When you start your horse's training it is tremendously important that you pay attention to the top line and how he carries himself. Some horses by nature will start with a high head on day one of the set period. I have started many horses that have come out of the field with a high head and hollow back. The first thing is, don't panic, but keep in mind you don't want to add to the problem. As long as there is no weight on the top line you have plenty of time to get the head and neck in the right position. The problems start in the top line when you jump on the horse's back with a shank bit and play cowboy at the rodeo. Playing cowboy at the rodeo teaches him to pop his head up like a goose in a cornfield.

The horse is like a computer. When you program the computer, good or bad, it's on the hard drive. On your home computer you have a pop-up blocker to help with unwanted messages. The young horse also gives you obvious unwanted pop-up messages. The main difference is you can clean up your computer and have pop-up guard protections. You don't have the same luxury with a horse.

It has been my experience that it is very difficult to re-train a horse that is confirmed with heavy-handed riding. If you think pop-ups are very annoying on the computer just wait until your horse learns to pop-up his head and hollow out because of heavy-handed riding. The truth is, when the horses are programmed with this approach some may never be re-claimed for pleasure riding. Why go down this road when you don't have to?

One main reason I use a 22-foot lunge rope is it puts less demands on the horse when walking the circle than the usual 12-foot lead rope.

Using a longer rope lets the horse use his body on a comfortable circle. By not putting a hard demand on the horse with a small circle you have a better chance of getting self-seeking reflex action of the head stretched out and down. When you start working the horse on the lunge, pay attention to the head and neck. At any time you observe the colt drop his head and stretch out and down (self seeking reflex action) give the colt a double reward by releasing the pressure on the face and a soothing voice of "good boy." Keep in mind, most colts will stretch the neck out and down with just playing on the lunge line. Just give them the time it takes and opportunity.

The walk is a four-beat gait. Each step is taken forward in an equal amount of time and space. The sequence is equal with each step before and after each leg movement. The cycle of one stride equals four even steps. When a horse is forced into a frame of high-headed, rude training the hollow back shuts down positive energy flow from the hindquarters. The horse's inability to relax his top line causes the four-beat gaits to fade away and drift toward ambling, pacing gaits. If the horse starts by nature with a high head and hollow back and the owner does not correct the problem you will also lose purity in the walking gaits.

When the horse is walking forward and the left hind foot lands on the ground the opposite right hind foot starts to swing forward. During this swinging phase is where I think the relaxation within the top line is so desperately needed. The hind leg swings forward and the head and neck go down to balance the motion. This is an alternating motion of relaxation coming from the hindquarters (through) with elastic push and pull. If at any time tension or stiffness is added to the top line on either side by poor riding or improper muscle tone you lose the even steps of the four-beat gaits. Knowing this motion is why I start my colts in a dog walk then into a flat walk. A good riding colt is a product of using a good set period with proper muscle tone development of the top line. Remember, I call the set period between the age of two and four years of age.

The walk is, and will always be, the most important gait. Why? Because this gait is the most stable to ride. The walk will reveal bad riding quicker than any other gait. In order to perform an evenly-timed gait the horse has to be relaxed on both sides of his body. The head and neck have to be allowed to lower (with head shake) in time with the hindquarters to develop the proper muscle groups. The dog walk and flat walk are an excellent gait to teach the Rocky Mountain Horses, Missouri Fox Trotters, Tennessee Walking Horses and Racking Horses prior to their individual finished gaits.

Review, write your own

Tasks:

Conditions:

Standards: Develop a relaxed top line in the horse at the ordinary walk and flat walk, maintaining a true 4-beat walk with the horse's head low, extended out from the withers.

Chapter Eighteen: The Running Walk

"In the matter of style, swim with the current. In the matter of principle, stand like a rock." Thomas Jefferson, 3rd U.S. President

The running walk has been described as poetry in motion. I have the opportunity to meet many different non-gaited horse owners at Equine Affairs all over America. When these owners see a Walking Horse for the first time the response is usually about how pleasing to the eye the running walk is to watch. It is very obvious they appreciate the beauty of the free flowing gait. The running walk is nothing more than a hint faster than the flat walk.

I enjoy talking to old timers who have trained and been around the running walk all their lives. They don't describe play-by-play movement of the gait, but rest assured they know what a good running walk looks like and also when it is not a good running walk. So far in this book I have stayed away from the five letter word which is speed. Most of our work has been with using a half halt into an upward transition from the dog walk or free walk into the flat walk.

The running walk is a free and easy moving gait that is a direct result of proper work that has been developed in the flat walk. The running walk is a hint faster with a more pronounced reach and rolling motion of the shoulders. I use the term a hint of speed here because, like the flat walk, form cannot be sacrificed for speed. It's been my experience if you start looking for the running walk without a good flat walk you stand a good chance of getting a good racking horse, especially if the horse has no natural reach. The running walk has to be a relaxed gait with drive from the hindquarters. Just like the flat walk, there is no room for stiffness and tension. Any tension in the top line will shut down the flow of energy in the horse's back. I cannot state this concept enough: The horse has to be relaxed with proper muscle tone to accomplish the running walk with proper form and timing.

The running walk is moving with a sense of purpose. You will see a deep headshake from the ears (poll) along the neck into the shoulders. The overstride can be as much as 24 inches or more. Most trail horses overstride around 14 inches. The overstride is the key element for a gliding smooth ride. A good running walk horse is like the energizer bunny, he keeps going and going. The running walk is a very efficient gait on the trail. The forelegs should move with a reaching elevated arc. The rear legs should drive under the horse's body with no wasted high hock motion.

A question one should ask is: What should we teach first, reach or break? The reach of the front end should be an elevated arc starting from the horse's shoulders. There should be no wasted up and down motion of the front legs. The leg should follow through as an extension of the shoulder. Reach is a component that is hard to teach. A top prospect

From the Trail to the Rail

horse with a good reach, in my opinion, has talent. You'd better look for this if you are in the show world.

The break is how high the knees lift off the ground. A trotting horse can break at the knees about level in an ordinary trot. Here's where it gets a little tricky. A good gaited horse gets about a 45-degree angle to about level using the front end. You want the knees at the same height, not off level, which is one knee higher than the other. It is very important you get the amount of break in the front end as a result of the drive of the hindquarters.

Now it stands to reason you don't need this much front end action on the trail. I'm only using a 45-degree angle plus as an example. The point I'm trying to make is the action (height) is a direct result of the hindquarters and energy flowing over the back. If you look closely at a trotting horse you will find the breaking in the knees is a result of the horse using the diagonal hind leg.

Now you have to make the call for pleasure riding. How much front leg action do you want and plan to ride? I love a good running walking horse breaking at the knees about level, good overstriding back end with a timed headshake. This is even too much for me on the trail. The remainder of this chapter is for the trail running walk horse. I'll discuss the society show horse more in a later chapter.

What is the standard for a trail running walk? For the quick look find a Walking Horse farm and watch the weanlings. The front-end actions on the colts are priceless. Take your video camera and film the weanlings. Watch the action in slow motion and commit it to your long-term memory. A word of caution, most babies have high heads. This will change with mixing and matching of gaits as the colt gets older. The horse is young and has the elasticity in his back that allows for this early high headset. Getting the right headset is one of the biggest challenges we face in training the horse. The horse switches gait too much.

It's very difficult to train for running walk without the same methods used in the flat walk. Matter of fact, if your horse cannot flat walk your running walk will suffer from lack of a foundation gait. Now, all things considered and your horse is doing a good flat walk we can start moving into the running walk.

Using a snaffle bit, ride on a loose rein to calm the horse's mind to get him ready for work. After about ten minutes of warm up, give the horse a half halt and move into a flat walk. Remember, the half halt is squeeze with your legs, catch with your hands, and release into gait. Impulsion is the drive from the hindquarters. Impulsion has very little to do with speed. To find the running walk from the flat walk we may have to try some different approaches. Every horse is different. We just need to put the puzzle together.

While in the flat walk give the colt a second half halt, feel if you get an accelerated motion. The motion has just become bigger with more headshake rolling out of his shoulder with more pronounced impulsion. That is in the perfect world.

Most of the time the horse, hopefully, will stay in the flat walk and that is fine. If the horse did not break into a pace or trot it is a good sign that you are on the right track. We just need to keep working towards the running walk.

This time, from the flat walk get your seat up more toward the withers. With your seat bones lightly touching the saddle, you're attempting to free the horse's back. If the colt responds and you get running walk, don't overdo it, give him plenty of praise and start developing an upward transition from the flat walk into a running walk. Don't freeze on the reins or pull back. These rein actions will put you on the forehand very quickly. One important point is to release into gait. Get the colt to work off the bit with a release. What I mean by a release is the colt is actively going forward with no pull on your hands and you are not pulling on his face.

Where you will get into trouble with an overactive hand is jamming the neck into the withers, causing the colt to fall onto the forehand. It only takes a short time to get the horse's neck jammed into the withers. This cause and effect is a result of poor hands and can go unnoticed for years. It does not take a very hard pull to get a jammed neck.

The running walk is extra smooth and gliding gait that is formed from the flat walk. The roll from the shoulders has the foot hitting on a heel to toe roll over. What I mean is in the flat walk the horse steps up and hits flat on his foot. In the running walk the horse hits the ground on the heel and quickly rolls off the toe. As the speeds increases so does the roll. Remember, form should not be sacrificed for excessive speed. If you ride your horse outside his headshake you are going too fast, more than likely starting to train a racking gait. As the speed increases the overstride also increases, maybe from six to eighteen inches. If you're into showing horses, the more overstride the better.

A good steady incline that requires the horse to shift his balance to the hindquarters can get the horse into a running walk. Start at the bottom of hill, half halt from the dog walk into a flat walk. Try just a little different spin on the next half halt. Squeeze the horse with your legs, now use your fingers to bump the reins which will bump the horse in the mouth. Now a little bump is far from a hard jerk. The bump in the mouth should come as soon as you feel the horse go forward. If the horse goes into a rolling motion with head shake you are in the ballpark. If the horse stays in the flat walk it's still what we want. It's not the end of world, we just have to keep working towards the running walk.

I know I'm repeating myself but the horse can go in so many different directions out of the flat walk that it requires a constant adjustment until

From the Trail to the Rail

he is set in gait. The bottom line is this, if you've got the flat walk working well the running walk will eventually develop. It's just a matter of time.

The barn is one of the best kept secrets in gaiting your horse. Ride in a dog walk around the barn for a few minutes getting the horse loose and relaxed. From the dog walk give the horse a half halt, ride away from the barn a couple hundred yards, stop and rest. Start the horse away from the barn again with a 'J'–turn back towards the barn. Make sure you give the half halt. Pay very close attention to how the colt is moving back to the barn, especially his speed. Ask yourself this question. Does he feel like he is moving with a sense of purpose? Often when going back to the barn/stall the colt moves with a sense of purpose to get done. He is not stupid; he knows where the comfort zone is located. You can trick him into a running walk because he wants to stop working on today's lesson. When you get to the barn don't stop, let the colt drop back into a dog walk for a few minutes.

Then, as before, give a half halt, ride a couple hundred yards away from the barn, stop and rest. Start again away from the barn, 'J'–turn with a half halt. Ride back to barn. Make sure your horse only rests away from the barn. You might be surprised how the horse will move with a sense of purpose.

Finding a sense of purpose can be fun with the horses. Now all I mean with the term "a sense of purpose" is he is moving like he's got somewhere to go in the flat walk, thus moving into the running walk, keeping his feet even in time, shaking his head, and overstriding the front tracks.

Try this experiment. It will be fun to go into the pasture field and feed your horse with a feed bucket. Use a regular feed bucket that he can eat out of easily. Watch how the horse moves toward the feed bucket. You can see the top line swell with pride and get level. The horse will square up into a running walk with a sense of purpose. Most of time, he'll be at the fence waiting for you. Get a friend to hold him still as you move about ten yards away and place his feed on the ground. Get off to the side to watch, then have your friend turn him loose and watch for the running walk with a sense of purpose. If the colt is breaking into a pace, trot, or canter, adjust the distance to less than 8 yards and watch again. If you're real serious about your experiment tell the horse what a good gait he is doing. Use your soft tone of voice as a reward for doing a good job. The horse will bridge every action together with feed as powerful motivator. I say this without reservation, I have seen more good running walk horses at feeding time than at any other time.

Again ask yourself this question: What happens to the horse's gait when we add weight to his back? Now I don't subscribe to the assertions that yesterday's horses were much more running walk horses. I will say we have lost some temperament in the gaited gene pool that would help on the trail. However, overall the gaited horses of today are very talented. What owners did many years ago that we don't do today was to ride the horse many miles a day in the flat walk until he found his running walk gait. Keep in mind, most horses will not square into gait until they have been worked about one hour. Now I don't advocate riding a two-year-old for an hour a day. I think this is too much on the skeletal system. To avoid overwork, play on the ground with the rope halter, and round pen work at liberty for about twenty to thirty minutes then ride slowly using the dog walk, flat walk into the running walk.

At trail riding camps I like to watch the owners ride out of camp onto the trails. Most of the riders return around lunch. I make it a point to be at the trailhead so I can watch the horses return to their campsites. You can see very quickly who has control between the horse and owner. With a 90% certainty I can pick which owners and horses will be at the afternoon clinic.

When the owners ride their horses out on the trail for about ten miles and then turn around a 1,000-pound flesh and bone missile heads back to camp, hell bent for leather. Again, the horse knows the location of the comfort zone (stall, hay, rest, and water). I call it the magnet pull with speed to the comfort zone. As the horse increases in speed his gait just gets lost in the speed shuffle. You will see pace, trot, and everything in between plus gaits that have not been identified. More times than not you have a hot, tense, firecracker of a horse. This behavior is not just in the gaited world. It goes to the very heart of the equine industry. The problem of rushing back to the trailers is not the end of world. I'll discuss how to solve rushing and use it to our advantage in the problem-solving chapter.

For now, just be concerned with walking the horse slow and flat into a running walk. Remember the old timer's saying, "The higher the horse's head the less brains, the lower the horse's head the more brains." This saying is so powerful it should be committed to your memory. I have my own saying, "a calm mind is terrible thing to waste with speed." Put your own spin on my saying, a running walk, fox trot, or four-beat self-carriage gait is a terrible thing to waste with speed. I hope by now you see that in the gaited trail world speed only plays a minor role. The more speed the more difficult the gait and the easier to fall onto the forehand. I receive e-mail after e-mail about finding the running walk gait. Teaching any gaited horse is relatively simple if you keep speed and balance in check.

Making general statements that a gaited horse requires too much work to get good gait is nonsense. When you add the weight of rider to any horse's back you have problems. You have to teach balance, not only to the horse but also to the rider.

Every now and then I get an e-mail saying we need a horse that is more set in his gait so the weekend riders won't have so much gaiting problems. I do have to agree with this assessment. Until then my response is, a horse is not a four-wheeler or a recreational vehicle. He has to be trained to exist with modern man, just like you as a child spent many hours hanging onto your mother's skirt.

There are a lot of nice gaited horses with good gene pools. Look closely for a good temperament horse which fits your trail horse needs. One the great sayings concerning the Tennessee Walking Horse, "Ride one today, own one tomorrow." is very true once you realize he is just like every other horse in the world. He has to be trained to do his job. It's the journey with leadership skills in training the young horses that makes the journey even more fascinating.

If you can achieve a finished horse in 90 days you need to be writing this book. Several years ago I received a blistering e-mail from a very knowledgable lady who wanted to know why a Tennessee Walking Horse needs a running walk when he was already doing a free walk and a flat walk. I e-mailed her back and asked why a farmer needs a tractor or a dressage horse needs a pure walk. I never heard from her again.

The breeds in this book are pleasure horses doing their pleasure gaits. A good temperament gaited horse is without question the world's best pleasure horse. The running walk gait is a pleasure to ride. The smooth, overstriding, headshaking, even gait becomes very comfortable to ride on the trails and on the rail.

Chapter Nineteen: The Missouri Fox Trotter

"Too much of a good thing is wonderful." Mae West

The Missouri Fox Trotter has been referred to as the "poor man's Walking Horse." I don't know who came up with this little saying. It's cute but very misleading. I'm sure there is some hidden meaning here. I'm going to give you my spin. The truth of the matter is a good Missouri Fox Trotter makes you feel like the "six million dollar man's Walking Horse" because

Dan'na's Magni, 4-year-old Missouri Fox Trotter stallion. Photo provided by Dyan Westvang, Foxvangen Farm.

his gaits are so smooth with a sensational glide for any owner, poor or rich. The Missouri Fox Trotter is trained in the flat walk as described in the previous chapters. There are no differences in training the young Fox Trotter in the flat walk as compared to the Tennessee Walking Horse, Rocky Mountain Horse, and Racking Horse. The Missouri Fox Trotters are trusting, curious, and eager-to-please trail companions. Hopefully you have established the dog walk (free walk) on a loose rein. The dog walk is the base camp for teaching the flat walk and then on to the fox trot. When teaching the fox trot, remember, the same old-timer rule applies, "The higher the horse's head the less brains. The lower the horse's head the more brains."

There are some very interesting movements that I have observed working with the fox trot in the last twenty years regarding the area of overstride that is unique to the Fox Trotter. This chapter centers on the upward transitions into the fox trot from the flat walk. The intent of the author for defining the fox trotting gait is for the old foundation Fox Trotting horse or ranch horse used in the Ozark Mountains for work and pleasure.

The gait of a Fox Trotting horse was developed for the needs of the footing in the Ozark Mountains. The ground is a mixture of limestone, sand ditches, and water gullies dotting the countryside. You also get cross sections of high mountain hilltops, valleys, spurs, and ridges. The need for a sure-footed, smooth riding horse is the result. This horse is equally suited to any terrain in the United States.

The fox trot is a diagonal gait with legs that support on opposite corners and therefore a sure-footed movement that supports a rider in rough terrain. A lateral going horse on a slick day can be a sliding experience. In the fox trot gait, the front foot touches the ground a split second before the opposite rear foot touches the ground. Now you heard this before with the running walk horse. "The front foot hits the ground a mere second before the hind diagonal opposite." Now the timing of a mere second and split second for the Fox Trotter is different than the timing of the four-beat running walk gait. The Fox Trotter's front foot touches the ground a split second before the opposite rear foot giving a unique rhythm and sound of a broken trot. The fox trot is a true diagonal gait because the horse breaks up the two-beat trot into a smooth, ground-covering gait. Most certainly other movements come into play. The hock action of a Missouri Fox Trotter has no wasted motion. The hock drives forward and helps create the smooth ride. There is no moment of bounce up and down in your seat with the fox trot gait.

Just like the Rocky Mountain Horse and Tennessee Walking Horse, you can push the Fox Trotter beyond his natural limits. The transfer of weight from the front foot hitting the ground a split second before the hind diagonal opposite lends itself to gait modification which will give many different variations seen in the show ring. Finding the balance point on the Missouri Fox Trotter is not difficult if the horse is ridden with rhythm, relaxation, and looseness. If it's worth saying I guess it's worth repeating, the young Missouri Fox Trotter must be worked slowly in a good snaffle bit to develop a calm mind, rhythm, looseness, and con-tact. The fox trot gait has a headshake in time with the hind feet. It is the counterbalance of motion behind the withers (mid point) that allows this colt to gait freely for miles with a smooth gait that is easy on both horse and rider.

Now keep in mind, if you were riding a trotting horse at the same speed as a fox trot you would be bouncing up and down in the saddle because of the fly time of the two-beat diagonal. The Fox Trotting Horse will support his weight using diagonal legs one side to the other while moving forward.

The musical trait of the fox trot I believe is rhythm. This broken diagonal gait has a defining sound. When riding on a gravel road you can hear the cadence, "A chunk of meat and two potatoes." Commit this sound to memory not only in your mind but also in the seat of your pants. The search to define the standard of how much break is needed in the diagonal of the fox trot has created controversy in the Fox Trotter show world. Remember, a hard trotting square horse is not a broken di-agonal gait. A trotting horse has diagonal pairs of legs working together. A pacing horse is not using a broken diagonal gait. Pacing is a two-beat gait with lateral pairs of legs leaving the ground at the same time on the same side.

Now here is where confusion hits Missouri Fox Trotters head on. The show world has stated today's Missouri Fox Trotter's stride is longer than his ancestors of years ago but the rhythm of a true fox trot has not changed. The statement sounds good but confusion rears its ugly head. You have controversy depending on who is listening to the broken part of the horse's trot, regardless of whether it is a first time owner or a seasoned trainer. Even seasoned veterans who have been in the Fox Trotter industry for years have difficulty agreeing with each other.

Again, I'm not picking on the show world, it has its place in setting some standards, but at what price should these standards change a smooth easy gaited horse? The questions all show industries have to answers is: When is bigger better? How much is enough? The good news is all of this confusion can be avoided by staying out of the horse's way and letting him do his job.

A Fox Trotting horse with a longer stride will come closer to a running walk. This type of horse you would call too slick (pace). A colt with a shorter stride tends to come closer to the square trot (too square). He may still be fox trotting but there is definitely too much bounce in your seat. He is not smooth. The ideal rhythm should receive more attention. In my opinion more attention should be paid to the timing of the feet with slow flat walk work. Finding the ideal rhythm is a tough concept when we ride too fast.

The headshake is in time with the rear feet. The rocking motion of the saddle is a result of the broken diagonal, when the timing is correct. You will feel a gliding motion in your midsection especially if you are seated just behind the horse's withers, which is the mid-point of balance.

What I mean by this is when the colt is flat walking, driving with his hind legs, and in time with a headshake, the stable area just behind the withers is sometimes called the sweet spot. If you seat yourself just behind this mid-point you can gently rock yourself to sleep. The horse has at least two feet on the ground at all times to support the rider's weight. The shoulder movement should move forward in a smooth motion and front foot sets down as an extension (reach) of the shoulder and front leg. The use of the shoulder with no wasted motion is a ground-covering gait. Feel how the colt is using his body in a total package. Feel for the rhythm.

The Missouri Fox Trotter is trained in a flat walk with an upward transition into the fox trot. Tack your colt with snaffle bit and a good fitting saddle. Don't get wrapped around the axles with shoeing. Bare foot or a good keg shoe will do just fine. Ride the colt with a loose rein, getting him relaxed and loose. To start developing the flat walk, remember the colt will have head shake, have 2 to 4 inches of overstride, and is even in gait. Using a half halt is to squeeze your legs, when you feel the horse surge forward catch with your hands, and release into gait.

Look for headshake and don't ride the colt outside his headshake. If you feel tension in the topline go back to free walk to establish relaxation and start again. You must have relaxation in order to get a good flat walk. Let the colt find a natural place to carry his head. Most of the time, this is just out from the withers. Just be patient and let this develop.

If you try to set the head too quickly you will jam the neck and get a racking motion in the front-end. During early training a snaffle bit should be considered in an effort not to put too much pressure in the colt's mouth. I believe a head set is a proper result of good riding. Now what I mean is to take your time and let a head set develop as a process, not a forced frame. The most movement you need now is to move the colt's nose two inches toward his chest. It will happen in time. For now, just be conscious of headset and see how many times you can achieve or capture the face without doing anything. Keep in mind if you want to start setting the head it's only a two inch movement towards the chest with most horses. Build the horse slowly.

Foxvangen's Solaris, 2-year-old Missouri Fox Trotter. Photo provided by Dyan Westvang, Foxvangen Farm.

Most horses will not have enough strength to flat walk without losing their balance. Go back and forth from a dog walk into a flat walk. Review chapters fifteen and sixteen on establishing the flat walk.

I am going to reiterate some concepts here because we are going from a flat walk into a fox trot, not into a running walk or pacing or trotting gaits. It's important you understand the flat walk gait. The flat walk is not a broken gait nor is it a two-beat gait (trot and pace). A good flat walk is a four-beat gait with each foot picked up and set down in an even time. In the flat walk each foot is stepping the same amount of time as the one before. The head shakes in time with the rear feet. The hindquarters should be smooth without high hock action. There should be no bounce in the tail, just smooth, soft, swing and flow. Each step is the same distance as the step before. In a good flat walk two and three feet are always touching the ground supporting the rider's weight.

The Missouri Fox Trotter is not hard to get into a fox trotting gait. They are bred to fox trot. The gait shifts into the fox trot from the flat walk using only small increments of speed. Just encourage your horse to increase his speed to hit the diagonals. Keep this in mind, with a Fox Trotter you want to flow into a fox trot. A simple half halt into gait can put you on the right track. I have some young horses that start fox trotting just from using my seat. Try to push the back of the saddle forward with your seat to encourage speed without overshooting the gait. Now what do I mean by overshooting the gait? The young horse will pick up speed, especially in his mind, and go too fast with his feet. Even though he seems relaxed he has a tendency to move his feet too quickly, beyond his foundation gait.

A young horse needs strength in the hindquarters to carry a rider in gait. A word of caution: Give the colt time to shift his mind from a four-beat walk into a broken trot. Now, if done slowly, it will be an automatic transmission change. If done without thought you can get ten different gaits.

I like to see the fox walk as a bridging gait. The fox walk, to some, is a little showier walk but a very useful tool to get into the fox trot. Just keep coaching for small increments of speed. Use your hands to bump the colt gently in the mouth, then release into gait when you feel the diagonal walk come together. You're now moving with a sense of purpose. Just keep building transitions back and forth. The colt will separate your intentions of what you're wanting but it does take time. Again, take the time it takes to develop smooth transitions for a lifetime of enjoyable trail riding.

Chapter Twenty: The Rocky Mountain Horse

"Always smile while you're riding, it changes your intent." James Shaw

The Rocky Mountain Horse is no stranger in Kentucky. These horses are sure-footed, easy to gait, and people friendly. During the 1800's to the latter part of the 1900's every day life in rural eastern Kentucky placed many different demands on the Rocky Mountain Horse. These horses could work farms, herd cattle, travel off steep rugged trails, and carry the mail. The Rocky Mountain Horse is extremely versatile and adapts to tough changing terrain in the Appalachian Mountain range.

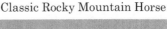

Classic Rocky Mountain Horse

As a young Kentucky State Police Trooper I was assigned to eastern Kentucky's London State Police Post. I become very fond of the Rocky Mountain Horses because of their versatility and temperament. Until the late 1980's most of the county roads were still gravel. Trail riding on Sunday afternoons was a popular pastime on these county roads. During many Sunday afternoon day shifts I would meet and watch the Rocky Mountain Horses traveling the county roads. What I remember the most is the smooth easy four-beat gait the Rocky Mountain Horses exhibited. What I observed the owners do with their Rocky Mountain Horses was ride them on long trail rides in a flat-foot walk. I watched the horses start at Mulling Station Road and I would monitor the same horses at end of a ten or fifteen mile ride. What I observed at the end of their ride was a foundation gait unique to the Rocky Mountain Horse. This horse is truly a reflection of the hard working people of eastern Kentucky.

Now I'm going outside the box to describe what I observed twenty-five years ago with this breed. As a matter of fact, with good basic horsemanship it's very easy to find this smooth four-beat gait just up from the flat walk. I am defining a pure walk. When you add a hint of speed you will find this pure walk with the Rocky Mountain Horse. The feel is a gliding sensation, freely going forward with powerful impulsion from the hindquarters. It is very comfortable to ride, but a word of caution, this balance can and will elude you if you add too much speed. Over-riding the horse into a stepping pace or rack will make it difficult to find what I'm trying to explain. The Rocky Mountain Horse is trained in a flat walk into a pure four-beat walk. The colt's hindquarters are genetically developed to allow the colt to perform a pure four-beat gait out of the flat walk. This horse was developed by hard working people who saw the value in working horses into gear from the flat walk. Their point of view was not to waste energy in a rack or stepping pace gait. The old farmer knew the horse had to work all day long to feed his family. These hard working people were able to consciously or unconsciously breed a horse for the right hock action to produce a pure self-carriage walk. Necessity is mother of all inventions. The good folks of the commonwealth in eastern Kentucky got this right.

The flash and bang of the show world is not what I'm describing as a four-beat gait. Without causing alarm to show barns, I'm not going to debate if the Rocky Mountain Horse is an ambling horse, which the registry by-laws suggest. The word ambling can become very misleading when describing the mid-range gaits. The term in the dictionary means an easy striding gait, suggesting a gait range anywhere from stepping pace to the country pleasure rack that is exhibited in the show ring.

Rocky Mountain Horses can be taught high, animated, stepping pace gaits for crowd-pleasing appeal, but at what cost to the horse and to the Rocky Mountain industry as a whole? Using running W's or other methods to get animation, a high front end, is putting this breed on same track as the Tennessee Walking Horse and Missouri Fox Trotter. Yet again I ask the same questions, when is bigger better? How much is enough?

Now, in my opinion, the highest form of excellence the Rocky Mountain Horse Association can ever obtain is smooth, overstriding four-beat gaits done in a keg shoe. "When much is given, much is expected." The breeders have to continue with breeding good temperament colts with four-beat gaits using foundation bloodlines.

In 1984, during the coal strikes in Pikeville, Kentucky, the Rocky Mountain Horses were ridden daily back and forth to the picket lines. Standing and guarding a bridge over the Tug River I watched the horses travel through the area. Again, what stands out in my mind is that the horses were ridden slowly in a flat walk then up into a four-beat gait with self-carriage. What great temperament they showed for their owners! During all the confusion and noise the horses never became rattle-headed. The horses took everything in stride as no big deal. The police and ambulances sirens and even tear gas never bothered them. Nary a time did I observe any refusal by the horse to obey the owner's request. Now look at this situation with a different spin. It's one thing to take your horse to a horse show, but to ride him into a full-scale riot and have him behaving, now that's priceless.

One more trip down memory lane. In the mid 1990's, I went to a Rocky Mountain Horse show in Lexington, Kentucky. As I recall, this was a National Championship show. What I observed in the early 1980's was a completely different gait than what I saw exhibited in that show ring. The vast majority of the horses at the show were in a stepping pace or a speed rack with the rider's feet resting on the dashboard. This was definitely a man-made, show gait. In one class a high-headed, step-ping pace, hollow-backed horse would tie. The next class a high-headed, hollow-backed, racking horse would win. Now don't get me wrong, if this is the standard the show world and trainers want to exhibit, the Rocky Mountain Horse lends itself to gait modification with the best of any gaited breed.

What I waited to see were the trail divisions. Guess what? In the trail divisions he stood out like a shining knight. The horse exhibited a nice even flat walk with an upward transition into a nice four-beat gait with self-carriage, working off his hindquarters. The riders on these horses were getting smooth, flowing rides with the horses moving forward with strong, driving hock action. I particularly paid attention to several ladies whose hair was tied in ponytails. There was no bobbing action or any movement that I thought would be an uncomfortable ride.

I watched three or four more trail classes and a sad truth reared its ugly head. The majority of these horses received no ribbon for doing a foundation gait. Now my trip down memory lane did not discourage me. I have since had the opportunity to work with many Rocky Mountain Horses year after year. Finding this wonderful evenly timed self-carriage gait is within the reach of all owners from novices to seasoned trainers. You can, with time, just flat walk your colt into gear.

Let me make myself perfectly clear, I'm not advocating a tail bobbing lick, stepping pace, country pleasure rack, rack, running walk, fox trot or other ambling gaits that a Rocky Mountain Horse is forced into for com-pliance with the show world. As long as the by-laws suggest an ambling gait as a Rocky Mountain Horse Association definition, the above gaits can be technically correct within the show world. The gait that I've come to observe is a four-beat gait just out of flat walk that is bold, four cor-nered, pure evenness, square, smooth, and exhibits a strong, independent, self carriage. The horse is so correct and balanced in his motion that it allows him to find self-carriage. Nothing with the horse's balance can be slighted or forced or a poor performance will result. I'm more than ever convinced that research in the future will isolate genes that are unique to this breed, not just a color.

Training the Rocky Mountain Horse in the flat walk is no different than training his cousins the Tennessee Walking Horse and Missouri Fox Trotter. The Rocky Mountain Horse will exhibit a trot and pace with all the mid-range gaits. Please refer to chapters 15 and 16 for training in the flat walk before you attempt to find the four-beat gait with self-carriage that I'm describing.

Now what is self-carriage? My definition is: A horse that can carry a rider using his hindquarters on a loose rein. The term collection is here in the sense that the horse will naturally collect his body still using loose-ness in an elastic sort of way without resorting to tension and stiffness in the top line. Keep this in mind the horse has to have strength to perform self-carriage. Two and three-year-old horses are not strong enough to maintain complete self-carriage but with time it develops nicely.

Look at it this way, you are in a holding pattern until any young Rocky Mountain Horse gets the strength to develop self-carriage. Take the time it takes in early training to assist the horse in developing his gait. Every now then you will feel some youngster move into the gait. Just reward him and be patient. When your horse is strong enough to carry your weight and is legged up, urge him on a notch above a good trail flat walk. This work can be done in snaffle bit offering tongue relief. I cannot overemphasize enough that the Rocky Mountain Horse has to be relaxed with a natural headset. For the most part, Rocky Mountain Horses exhibiting a high head will drift towards a stepping pace or racking gait.

The term "natural" can mean many different areas where a horse can carry his head. There are naturally high-headed horses and naturally low-headed horses. Keep the horse's head elevation just out from his withers without any hollowing of the horse's back caused by the rider's bad seat, poor hands, or over-bitted horse. If you have trouble with this concept, get professional assistance.

What you are looking for, and more importantly what you want to feel, is when the horse has activated his hindquarters. When training for the self-carriage gait your goal is to shift the horse's balance point to the hindquarters. The horse is going to move with a sense of purpose. The overstride will be somewhere around 18 inches, more or less. The forelegs should move with a reaching, elevated arc. The hind legs drive under the horse's body with no wasted hock motion. Keep working from the flat walk with an upward transition into the four-beat gait for self carriage. Work slowly. Don't try to force the gait, just let it happen.

You can best feel what I'm advocating if you find a creek with about 12 inches of water. Feel how the horse moves in the water and uses his body. This is the same exact feel I want you to teach the horse on flat, dry surfaces. For safety reasons don't use a tie down when working horses in water.

Develop into transitions from the dog walk into a flat walk and then a self-carriage walk. The name of the game is walking. Speed has no place at this time. Don't despair, speed will come with time, but for now your horse needs to know where to put his feet and get the transitions down in his mind. You can call this playing the slow scale. Say to yourself, how slow can I go? Or how much slower can I go to get independent movement of the feet?

Just like with the running walk horses, ask: How much break and reach should the colt have in the front legs? The answer is found watching well-bred weanlings. Film the weanlings and pay particular attention to their movement in the flat walk. You will see just a reach out of the

From the Trail to the Rail

shoulders in time with his hind foot. There is no wasted motion in the hocks or shoulders. Everything moves forward as a complete movement with the front foot as an extension of the timing from the hindquarters. Common sense suggest that a reaching colt going forward in a keg shoe will achieve a rear end balance much easier. In my opinion, this is why the mountain farmers in Kentucky were able to walk the horse into gait. They did nothing to destroy the natural balance with too much break in the knees. With the Rocky Mountain Horse the action in the front end is a result of the action from the rear hindquarters. You, as the owner, will have to decide how much front-end action you need on a good trail horse.

Try this method with your Rocky Mountain Horse. Ensure your horse is legged up and sound. This exercise is for a horse four years old or older. Just using a plain snaffle bit, head for some moderate trails, nothing extreme at this point. Ride the horse slowly for a minimum of two hours. Walk the horse as slow as you can just in an ordinary walk. If he goes into a flat walk slow him back down. Go as slow as you can for about two hours. Just feel the motion of the feet and how slow you can time the feet. See how long it takes for the feet to separate into a four-beat timed gait. Now, with a half halt just urge the horse forward and feel the flat walk gait. Add another half halt and coach the horse into a four-beat self-carriage gait. This is the same movement with the feet but no headshake. Don't let the horse go into a stepping pace or a slow style rack. Just stay slow in gear and feel the old-timer's lick. This gait will feel the same as when you were walking in water. The key to this horse is to walk him slowly into gait. Keep adding speed in small increments until you can get into a six to eight miles per hour range. This is a good horse that only needs slow and flat training.

To clarify some misconceptions about Rocky Mountain Horses being labeled single-footing horses or racking horses, this is stepping outside the foundation boundaries of the breed's intended purpose. Read carefully below the Single-Footing Horse standards below. If you can ride your Rocky Mountain Horse at the speeds listed below, or the flying stepping pace seen in the show ring today you can only be riding a mutated gait for show pleasure, not the original foundation gait intended for the Rocky Mountain Horse.

According to the North American Single-Footing Horse Association definition of single-footing:

"What makes the single-footing gait unique? Ideally the gait is an intermediate 4-beat gait and is very nearly even in timing. It can be performed at a huge range of speeds, from a relaxed trail speed of 7 to 9 mph, to a ground eating road gait speed of 12 to 15 mph, to the breathtaking racing single-foot (and the speed at which the name 'single-footing' comes from) of over 20 mph. At the fastest speeds these horses will be traveling with one foot on the ground at a time, thus the name 'single-footing'. Some horses will start single-footing

at a road gait speed and others at racing speed. Either is correct. While the ideal horse will remain as close as possible to even timing at all speeds, the reality is that at top speeds these horses tend toward a more lateral timing. We do not want to see horses that are near a dead pace at speed and do not consider this single-footing. Speed is characteristic of this gait, but speed at the intermediate gait for the sake of speed with improper form is not a goal. This makes for a weak-gaited saddle horse and that is exactly what NASHA wants to avoid. Locating the few remaining pockets of horses with a true single-footing gait was not easy. When found, these horses were generally very tightly line-bred. Outside blood was necessary. For the first several years any horse with an intermediate 4-beat gait was eligible for registration as long as the owners were dedicated to producing single-footing horses from that point on. The registry is still open but in 1998 horses that running walk, fox trot, slick pace, or have extremely long striding, or short tight striding gaits are no longer accepted for registration. The registry will place appropriate restrictions on new applications to ensure overall quality and correctness of gait."

The bottom line is, a Rocky Mountain Horse is a four-beat gait horse with ordinary walk into flat walk then into a four-beat walk that is defined by self-carriage. The Rocky Mountain Horse will use his feet like the running walk horse but without a headshake. When he drifts towards the rack he tends to become too lateral. This particular horse lends itself to gait modification for wide variations of gaits. The industry is still growing by definitions but not evolving. The gait I'm describing has always been there for any owner who will take the time to let the horse develop in regards to his natural, genetic abilities. There will always be barns that promote this type of horse I'm describing using old bloodlines. Please consider temperament and the intent of the founding breed history in selecting a good Rocky Mountain Horse for your trail or rail needs.

Chapter Twentyone: The Single Foot Rack

"The feet don't lie." Gary L. Lane

The rack is a natural gait that strongly shows itself within the Tennessee Walking Horse, Missouri Fox Trotter, and Rocky Mountain Horse breeds so it would be impossible to write a book about training these breeds without talking about the Racking Horse gaits. A whole industry is built around the rack. Let's start with a definition of the rack in the sense of a using gait. Keep in mind the single-foot rack is a wonderful gait to ride and a pleasure to look at if ridden correctly.

The rack of the Racking Horse is a bi-lateral four-beat gait, which is neither a pace nor a trot. It is often called a single-foot because only one foot at a time strikes the ground. One foot supports the horse while three feet have a moment of suspension. The rack must not exhibit exaggerated headshake, curling front end, or high hock action. The stride should be steady and long with a natural reaching front-end action. Note it is the author's belief that speed and head elevation can affect the rack causing several different racking gaits depending upon the headset and back position.

With this definition in mind one must ask some questions: What is the difference between a rack and a flat walk? What is the difference between a rack and a running walk, a fox trot, and a self-carriage gait? The answer to these questions lies within the above definitions. The rack is a very smooth natural gait occurring most of the time when speed is added to the formula. It would be a fair statement to say speed and head elevation are defining ingredients in obtaining the racking gait.

Keep in mind when a foot is on the ground you can say that foot is in a support phase. When a foot is off the ground it is a suspension phase (fly time). Within the gaited horse world there are many variations of the support phase and suspension phase. The term single-foot rack means only one foot is on the ground in a support phase and three feet are off the ground for a mere second in suspension phase or fly time. All this is done within one stride, which is only four foot falls. It takes time to train your eye to see this suspension with three feet off the ground.

If you start your count of the gaited horse's stride with the left rear foot as step one (first beat) the left front foot is the second beat. When you add speed you will get three feet off the ground momentarily before the right hind

foot hits the ground as the third beat. The sequence of one foot on the ground for support and a mere second of suspension with three feet off the ground is a single-foot rack. When the feet move in this manner most horses have a very limited headshake because the horse just does not have enough time to shake his head. The speed of the gait is outside the horse's ability to shake his head.

Now here is the great mystery we need to understand. Without planning to, you can get a headshaking horse with the feet moving in a Racking Horse phase of one-foot support and three feet off the ground. Just for fun take your video camera and film a horse show or watch horses on-line. Slow the video down and look closely at the foot movement. With just one foot supporting and three in suspension a strong argument can be made that this type of horse is racking with a deep headshake. You see this movement with a squared up pace or a squared up stepping pace often called a man-made running walk or man-made walk. Now it is, what it is.

A good friend of mine, Allanna Jackson, who is one of the top three people in the nation in the science of equine gait identification, would look at a photo and say the horse is racking. Now I would take the same photo and see a perfectly good running walk. What she so cleverly let me find out for myself is that the footfall pattern and support of the feet cannot lie or be altered without affecting the horse's balance. Her gait research, begun in the early 1980's, clearly shows the difference between earlier horses and the gait modification we see today. You must remember the feet don't lie. I credit Allanna Jackson for being one of the first people I've met who has gone down this road of understanding the truth about gait modification which may be her greatest contribution to the gaited world, only time will tell.

The feet don't lie. Let's look at the Tennessee Walking Horse breed with genetic markers for gait modification. Industry leaders are not off the hook. Somebody is going to have to explain in gait science to owners why we are so far away from an even gait as was seen with Walking Horses in the 1940s.

The running walk horse that was seen in early 1940's would running walk with two and three foot support on the ground. There was no fly time with suspension (meaning three feet off the ground). Sadly, not many of these horses are left today. Maybe a few are scattered west of the Mississippi River and in Canada. If you are lucky enough to own one of these horses you will not experience the gait modifying problems seen with the modern horses bred for high headed, hollow backed movement. It's fair to say that in the process of breeding to create a more crowd pleasing performance lick we have lost some genetic markers that would have made life a lot easier when it comes to gaiting your horse.

Keep in mind there are two schools of thought. One group supports a squared up pace and stepping pace horse for gait modification into a man-made lick and another group supports a traditional-gaited horse for pleasure to present to the American public requiring little or no gait modification. Both groups are passionate that they are right about the future. Very little common ground is found with both groups. Arguments just add more confusion to the mix. It now appears that the Rocky Mountain Horse and Missouri Fox Trotter are on the same road. In my opinion in our zeal for more performance we forgot to ask the horse what's in his best interest. The welfare of the horse should always come first and foremost. This is where the correct answer is found for the future of all the breeds mentioned in this book. Any other standard will fall far short in controversy.

Now it stands to reason in order to get flat walk and running walk you have to ride the horse slowly with proper head elevation. In my opinion, slow flat-foot walking will get the horse working off the hindquarters to develop headshake.

One of the reasons I advocate the flat walk is it is a safe, sure-footed gait for the trail. I like the concept of riding a horse slowly and letting the horse develop within his own time frame. This does not require any special shoeing or gait modification. Just ride with what's underneath you slowly and look for your headshake.

Here again the flat foot walk is the key to developing the modern day horse to obtain a good headshaking gait with independent leg support. Keeping the feet on the ground with two and three feet in support is the old running walk, which required little gait modification. The front end should be clipping the grass. Riding for hours on a loose rein in a slow flat foot walk with proper (low) head elevation will solve many problems with the modern day horses.

Many Missouri Fox Trotters will also slip into a rack when ridden too fast and exhibit less headshake. He will support his body with one foot on the ground with three feet off the ground in fly time. When a Fox Trotter starts racking he moves away from broken diagonal foot movement into a lateral slick foot movement. This often creates a trappy front-end look with wasted up and down movement. The cure is the same as for the Tennessee Walking Horse, slow the horse down. Give him time to separate his feet and shake his head in a good diagonally timed fox trot.

Now keep in mind a good Racking Horse does not exhibit wasted front-end motion with a straight up and down motion of the front legs. A good single-foot Racking Horse uses his hindquarters with a nice easy reach in the front end.

The Rocky Mountain Horse with the old bloodlines did not singlefoot rack in the self-carriage gait (four beat gait). The old Eastern Kentucky horses supported their movement with two or three feet on the ground with independent leg movement. In the flat walk the old Mountain Horses had a very noticeable headshake. When moved up in speed the Rocky Mountain Horse exhibited an independent four beat gait with limited headshake. There was no fly time with three feet coming off the ground and one foot in support. Riding too fast has also come to the Rocky Mountain Horse.

The rack gait does have a place in history with gaited horses. You can get a nice slow rack if you give the horse time to develop the gait, which is a joy to ride. I just question the wisdom of taking a nice country pleasure racking gait and riding the horse too fast with a high head, hollow back and long shank bit. This type of riding can cause mental and physical problems with sensitive horses. Taking the time to watch the sequence of footfall and how the horse supports his body with his movement will go a long way in deciding which gait you want to ride on the trail or rail.

Chapter Twentytwo: Problem Solving the Pace and Re–training on the Ground

"It is the very difficult horses that have the most to give you." Lyndon
Gray

Problems in the flat walk can present themselves in a wide variety of
ways depending on the situation. Just starting a young horse can present
a very different set of problems than buying a horse from a training barn
presents. Everything depends on the situation, the horse, and your ability
to recognize the problems. Problems can vary from the mouth, saddle
fit, rider inexperience, shoeing, medical problems, mental problems, and
genetics. The horse can present problems with the pace, trot, or a combination of both. The procedures outlined in this book will solve many
problems if followed with the tasks, conditions, and standards training
format in the young horse.

A wide range of problems can manifest in colts from show training
barns where they were started as big-lick horses and did not make for
some unknown reason. You should also realize many colts are culled each
year for the public auctions and private sales that did not make as Missouri Fox Trotter show colts, or Rocky Mountain Horse show colts. The
culled show horses are what I call a more specialized training problem
because of the shotgun training they've had. These horses present a wider
range of problems than farm raised colts that develop a back yard attitude. You must realize training barns are commercial enterprises, intent
on making money quickly. Often only the best of the best are kept for
training for the show world. I believe more show horses would make if
given more time with the mental side of the horse. Trying to train a colt
in 90 days with advanced collection is nonsense.

Now as long as people exist they are going to show something,
whether it is horses, dogs, cattle, or sheep. Considerations about showing
a horse are the ethical obligations to train with sound principles which
make the horse's welfare a higher prioirity than winning. The horse has
to accept his training and be calmer after the lesson. Keep in mind, the
horse can't be hurt, the trainer can't be hurt. I can say more and more
training barns are using good sound training techniques, producing some
nice horses and taking the time it takes to get the job done right.

The best way to re-train or solve problems is to act like a police detec-
tive. You first have to identify the problem, leave nothing to chance,
determine how confirmed the problem is, and take action to solve the
problem. Ask yourself some questions: Am I committed to solving the
problems? Do I need professional help? Will I stay committed to solving the problems? Remember, there is no shame in asking for help.

The remainder of this chapter will address gait related problems. There
are basic common problems with all breeds such as bucking, shying,
standing still to mount and dismount. All these behaviors have to be

taken into consideration with the horse's training or re-training. There are many good people out there today who can assist with basic common problems. These matters are important and have to be resolved. For example, if you can't mount the horse you can't gait him.

In dealing with gait problems, and at risk of boring you, I will have to repeat and emphasize already addressed training methods. The best way for me to teach you something is to tell you in small steps of training and then tell you again and again. Remember, you are the one who has to turn on the light bulb and grasp the main idea.

In re-training a problem horse I use three concepts. (1) Identify the problem. (2) Discuss the problem developing a training plan using tasks, conditions, and standards. (3) Take action to solve the problem.

Believe it or not, the hard part is to identify the problem. When you get to the root cause you have won half the battle. Success or failure rests with you having the self-discipline to resolve the problem. These three concepts can be adapted to use with any problem you encounter with a horse. A good plan today is worth a perfect plan tomorrow.

The pacing colt is the number one problem that requires more of my attention than any other area of gait problems. There are several areas we need to address regarding the pace. When the walk drifts toward a pace with one side of horse picking up both feet on the same side in unison, then the other side in unison, the beat becomes a two-beat gait. It has been my experience that for the  majority of horses the cause is tension in the top line. Most of the time the cause is the horse has been forced into a frame before it is ready. The pacing movement usually accompanies a high head and hollow back.

Sometimes, but not always, the horse does not want to slow down. The horse gives the impression he is running away from pain. Riding a horse too fast, outside his ability, does nothing to diminish the pace.

Everyone has heard, "A pacing horse needs weight in the front and light in the rear." This old concept has been around for years but it is misleading because too much weight can cause a labor pace that leads to the same aforementioned problems. The weight concept gives the idea that all that is required to square the colt is weight. The weight adds more difficulty in squaring the horse into a four-beat gait, changing the degree of reach into up and down motion.

Mouth tension is the result of too much shank and will cause a pace in the walk. Mouth tension can show up in a slow labor pace motion, but not all the time.

A poor fitting saddle can cause a pace walk and can be accompanied with behavior problems.

The age of the horse can be a factor, especially a young horse in the set period that has not yet developed a good sound top line. Not having enough strength to carry a rider can and will cause pacing problems.

A Walking Horse that has been on pads or ridden in a full package has to have the top line developed into a square gait. When a padded horse is returned to a natural way of going this usually exposes pacing problems. The list is not conclusive and many more factors can be present. To solve the pace you have to cure the pace by developing the top line.

In re-training a horse, look at the background of the horse and find out as much information as you can. Find out who started the horse. There is nothing wrong with contacting the trainer. Try to find out if the horse was paced out prior to culling. This usually is a period of a month or more of hard pacing. Try and find out why the horse was culled. Was he too slick? Was he too square? Ask the prior trainer if any old videotape exists of the colt under saddle. Now is a good time to have a friend videotape you riding your horse under saddle for further evaluation. All this information adds up in a base cluster and gives you a road map on where to start.

There is nothing wrong with having a good vet examination. Pay particular attention to the top line looking for back pain and the mouth for scar tissue. Don't forget about a good equine dentist.

After you have decided the horse is pace walking or has a natural tendency to drift towards the pace, go ahead and have the horse shod in a keg shoe. I recommend a good balanced foot in front with no shoes on behind. Your goal now is to develop the top line for balanced movement with an even gait, head nod, and overstride.

Pay attention to basic needs such as, can you mount and ride the colt safely? Are there any basic problems that need immediate attention prior to re-training for an even gait?

Commit to your long-term memory the words pain, fear, excitability, and muscle tone. These four areas are all key areas that require balance in the horse's life.

Prior to re-starting the training program turn the horse loose in the field for a month or so just to let him be a horse. Establish a feeding program where he can develop trust in you. During this period don't ask for anything other than trust between you and the horse. The training below is recommended for Tennessee Walking Horses, Missouri Fox Trotters, Rocky Mountain Horses, and Racking Horses.

Start the horse on the ground with a 22-foot lead rope to develop trust and a calm mind. There is no difference in this re-training and the training outlined in chapters 4 through 9. Please refer back to those chapters for re-training. During this training period or re-training period it appears the training is proceeding much faster than when starting a new horse. Here is where mistakes are made with good intentions. Don't get fooled. He has to have a calm mind in order to develop the top line to rid the horse of pace problems. Training for a calm mind cannot be slighted or second-rate performance will be obtained. If you can't get the horse to relax in his mind you cannot develop the top line. Some horses will act calm on the outside but are very nervous on the inside. Remember, he has already been programmed. You have to clean the hard drive and start over. There are no quick fixes, just good old-fashioned slow work.

The hard part of re-training is to recognize the flash back. What I mean by this is, everything is going great when, with or without provocation, the horse flashes back to his previous training. Most of the time this is a high head and hollow back coupled with a pacing problem. A good indicator of good re-training is to monitor the flash backs. They will become less and less in training. For example, the horse may have three or four flash backs a day to once a week then once a month. You overcome the flash back problem with consistent training on the ground and in the saddle. You have to be patient and observe how the horse reacts to pressure. If he blows a fuse every time you ask for something, slow down and be consistent.

It has been my experience when re-training horses that the word consistent is the key to success. With re-training a horse you are going back and starting over with the colt's mind and body. You have to fill in the parts of the foundation that need shoring up. More times than not, key training points were jumped with shotgun training methods. All you are doing is going back and fixing up the parts that were missed.

One concept that has helped me over the years in re-training a horse is finding the base line. What I mean is, what is normal behavior for this horse? Understand his behavior when he is calm and relaxed. Get a good feel of calm behavior on the ground, especially observing the horse's body language. Very slowly ask for a request, say lunge to the right. Now observe, at what point during the request did the horse blow a fuse? How much pressure on the hip could be put on the horse before he steps out of his normal, calm base line behavior?

The spoiled horse has already been programmed with stiffness and tension in the top line. When re-training this type horse you have to find the base line to keep the horse relaxed. Then with small increments of pressure work up to how much pressure can he take? How little pressure does it take? The goal is to get the horse trained with just a slight suggestion.

I have found many horses that shut down inside their minds. These horses appear relaxed but have mentally shut down with human handling. This horse can be a real challenge. Shutting down is a self-protective response to the fear, tension, and confusion created by shotgun training methods. This type of horse is very likely to surprise you with a flash back, or blow a fuse and use all the bad habits he has learned to protect himself if you go too fast, even when you think you are going slow. In time, with slow patience and kind training, a horse of this type may recover and you will be amazed at his true personality.

During the ground work getting control of the hindquarters is a must to defuse the horse's power. Get a good crossover with the inside hind leg crossing over the outside hind leg. Develop the rear-end-under and the front-end-across. There can be no room here for a gray area. The work has to be consistent. The lighter you get the horse with this movement the easier it is to develop his top line to solve the pace.

During re-training use the ground work period to teach the horse to lunge both ways and cause the horse to separate the front end from the hindquarters. Watch and determine if the horse drops and stretches his head out and down with the rope halter. This is a good sign. Make sure you give an immediate reward for his efforts.

Remember, all horses will do a regular walk regardless of breed. It is best to try this walk in a round pen, or a small 25 foot by 25 foot enclosure. A barn hallway works fine. Walk your horse on a loose lunge rope, no pulling on his face. Walk off slightly to the rear at an angle to the horse's hindquarters. Think of driving the horse with one line walking off to the side.

Just find a nice dog walk with the lunge line. When doing a dog walk you are not concerned with a headset. The horse needs to relax and be allowed complete freedom to stretch out and down with his head and neck. Using the lunge rope, keep soft contact on the face. From the ground you can see a loose swing with the tail like a pendulum back and forth. When the horse is in this position we are starting to develop the top line to cure the pace. Pay attention to the relative head and neck position when the horse is dog walking. The muscle groups work together, as a hind leg swings forward the head and neck go up. As the same leg pushes off the ground the head and neck move down. This is an alternating motion with both sides of the horse's body. This is a good exercise in solving pacing problems. It lets you see exactly what you have to do under saddle.

If you can get this free walk working for you on the ground it is definitely a short cut in re-training. Take full advantage of this ground work. Stay with this exercise as part of the horse's daily training. I would go so far as to say the dog walk must become part of the horse's new life style.

Most of the time you will get a horse that will want to run off and not listen. Remember, in his previous training he has had his tail pushed through the bridle. It is very easy for him to become excited. Keep in mind pain, fear, excitability, and muscle tone is an ongoing process of development. Let the horse run into the lunge rope and roll the hindquarters to defuse the power and start over. Just keep presenting what you want but you must remember it's about the horse understanding what you want and you having the patience to give him time to understand. In your mind always be ready to reward with a release when you see the desired behavior. It has been my experience most horses find the behavior you want by accident so be ready at all times with a release - reward. There is no set time frame, just take the time it takes.

Most re-training consists of horses that don't want to drop their head and horses that hollow their back. I use (cavalletti) ground poles. Place four poles about 15 feet apart in a small round pen or other small 25 foot by 25 foot enclosure. The picture above isn't in an enclosure so you can see what's going on better. I use a 22-foot lunge rope. Using the clock method, place one pole at 12 o'clock, one at 6 o'clock, one at 3 o'clock, and one at 9 o'clock. You stand in the center circle using your body and lunge rope to put pressure on the horse's hip. At first don't worry if the horse does not walk across all the poles in the direction you are working. Get him going forward and let him step over one or two and then he will dodge one or two, just go forward.

Keep this in mind, what the horse does before he walks across the poles or dodges is what you are looking to observe. As the horse walks over the pole he will slow, sometimes even stop to look and lower his head. When you see the horse start to drop his head this is the time to reward and take pressure off the horse's face. Stay with this exercise. He will get the message and walk over all the ground poles. This is demanding exercise. Don't overtax the horse. Do it about three or four times a week working up to 15 to 20 minutes with dwell (stop) time.

You will find some horses will not slow down. Some seem to use this as a trick to drag the owner around all over the farm. Some of this charging ahead behavior could be exciteable temperament, hard wiring to pace, flashing back under saddle, or even a desire to please. I can say this without reservations, I like the horse that goes forward without request. A little hint of this is where the horse's show gait is located.

On the ground with this type of horse I like to go to the woods with a 22-foot lead rope. The reason I like to use a 22-foot rope when working a gaited horse is it allows for the opportunity to let the horse find a re-laxed walk. The large circle puts less demand on the horse's legs and gives him greater freedom in using his body to develop the walk. Try to find a stand of trees that are spaced about three or four feet apart. I have de-signed a little corner of wooded area on my farm for this purpose. I have had a many of my students and horses go to the woods for re-training. In the woods just let the horse train himself. He will charge off as usual, but every time the lunge rope touches a tree just hold. The horse will roll the hindquarter over and face you. Let him take off the other way. He will meet a different tree and get to roll his hindquarters over and face you again. The horse is no dummy, he gets the message very quickly to start listening to you. I like playing a little maze game to see if the horse can find his way back to me. One thing to look for is when the horse wants to stand with you and not charge off. He is getting the message.

The only horse this ground play will not help is the horse that will not go forward. Just get a flagstick and you can solve the little problem of sticking with the feet. Most horses that buck under saddle are the ones who start out not wanting to go forward. These horses stick their feet on the ground and refuse to go forward. Then when they do go forward they want to suck the ground with their nose and buck. This is nothing more than a refusal to go forward. Getting control of the hindquarters will stop most of this behavior. This usually involves a farm-raised colt with an attitude.

Getting the pacing horse to work with a low headset and looking where he is going is the purpose for my use of an obstacle course. The key point to remember is to direct the horse over the obstacle course. Stand off to the rear and direct the horse from the hind-quarters to negotiate the obstacle. When you do this he thinks it is his idea to step on or over the obstacle. The obstacle course takes on the concept of getting your horse to do your thing his way the best he can. Refer to chapters on ground-work and starting the colt over obstacle courses for a calm mind.

The walk with relaxation has to come first with gaited horses. After the walk has been established using the 22-foot rope, spiral the horse in closer to you by taking up 8 feet of lunge rope. Let the horse trot around you. This is a great exercise to develop the top line and not place hard demands on the horse's back while re-developing the top line. After a few minutes of trotting let the horse spiral back out into a dog walk. The trot is a fine working gait when not under saddle. The trot is a difficult gait to master under saddle without hurting the horse's back. Go to any dressage show in America and look at the poor horses' backs getting beat like a jackhammer. No wonder this industry has an alarming amount of unsound horses.

Everything we have done so far on the ground is designed to strength-en the horse's top line into a more round frame to carry himself, elimi-nating the position of a high head and hollow back. Some horses are wired so tight it will be a challenge to get the horse's head down and back round. There is nothing wrong with seeking professional help with this type of horse. The conditioning of a horse is an art within itself. Some horses with a winter off will start back in spring with a pace or stepping pace gait. After a few rides the horse squares back up into the desired gait. It's been my experience, when a horse is doing a square even flat walk with overstride and head nod he likes doing his gait and becomes very sporty in using his body. The horse realizes it is much easier to carry a rider from the rear forward and will tune into the gait and get better and better with a light front end.

Task: Teach the horse to square from a pace into a flat walk (devel-oped top line.)

Conditions: A slow walk in all types of terrain and under all weather conditions.

Standards: A good flat walk is a four-beat gait with an even footfall, the horse nods his head with an overstride.

Chapter Twentythree: Problem Solving the Pace
Under Saddle

"Too much haste just adds problem with the pace." G. L. Lane

When you start to re-train a horse there most certainly will be times when you need to correct a horse with a high head and hollow back. If you use a ten-inch shank bit to disengage the hindquarters you're not correcting anything. Most of the time you will get an overreaction from the pain in the horse's mouth. Just a few overreactions can and will lead to all sorts of behavioral problems. I see this time and time again, horses showing signs of resistance on the trail or the rail. You must have good soft contact to calm the horse's mind, which will solve many training problems.

I get the opportunity to work with many problem horses. I can honestly say heavy contact with too much bit leads to a high-headed hollow-backed horse and a pacing horse. The reason I repeat this information is to say the same thing in a little different way to turn on a light bulb. I am more than ever convinced that gaited horses need training in classical lightness.

Now to cure the pace, I highly recommend a combination bit. The only way this bit won't help you is if you don't use it. Most horses that need to be re-trained have already been exposed to a bit, whether good or bad. The point is you now need a bit that does not cause flash backs and pop ups (high head and hollow back). This combination bit disperses your rein pressure, allowing you to work off the nose, poll, and chin and ride the horse from the withers for a rounded position that will develop the top line. The good part is the horse learns how to carry the bit in his mouth all over again without causing tension in his mouth, resulting in a pacing gait. Now there is big percentage of (usually) older horses whose mind will calm quickly when there is no bit pain. If you don't have a combination bit a good tongue relief bit will work fine.

Right now stay away from shanks bits until trust is established. I like the concept, with a spoiled horse, of using tongue relief bits. It's been my experience some horses never got past tongue pressure in learning to carry the bit in their mouth. They just seem to hang with tension in the mouth, giving the owner all sorts of problems. When you get a calm mind and a comfortable mouth you have a good starting point to train or re-train your horse. One of the things you want to guard against is any action from the rider that causes a pop-up of the horse's head and neck.

It's the rider's responsibility to ensure that the saddle fits and does not causes any pain, fear, or excitability. The saddle should lay flat on the horse's back with no rocking back and forth. The stirrups should hang down directly under the saddle in a straight line, not offset forward or offset to the rear. Getting good professional help with saddle fit is just good sense.

The best place for the rider to sit in re-training is just behind the withers up off the pants pockets. This seat has been referred to as the old cowboy seat. Make sure you do not roll backwards onto your pants hind pockets. It's very important you stay up off the horse's back. The location here is sometimes called the sweet seat. Why? This position is over the horse's center of gravity and allows you more options with the aids. It also takes weight off the horse's back for a clean start in training.

Prior to mounted work it's important that you spend some time on the ground with the bit in the horse's mouth and saddle on his back. The reason I waited to add this concept here with the horse tacked up is because the training is more effective just prior to riding. The goal is to build trust with the bit in his mouth and the saddle on the back. Please refer to Chapter 15 Teaching The Flat Walk.

With re-training a spoiled horse it's imperative this horse gets more sacking out (de-sensitizing) time with the riding crop all over his body. The goal is a relaxed, total acceptance of the riding crop. Prior to mounting each day stand on the ground close to the shoulder of your horse. Use your riding crop and start rubbing the crop all over the horse's body. The goal is to de-sensitize the horse so you don't get an over-reaction when you tap the horse to go forward.

Now stand on the left side of your horse's head. Use your left hand on the inside rein to gently lift the bit up and down in the horse's mouth. Vibrate with your fingers or use a very gentle shaking motion. Look for a response that the horse is moving his tongue up and down under the bit and starting to chew. This response indicates the horse is relaxing the poll behind the ears.

Now, move the horse's head two to four inches to the left toward you. Use your riding crop in your right hand to gently touch the horse's hindquarters. When the horse takes a step with the inside hind leg, pay attention to the elevation of the horse's head. When he starts to drop his head, release and follow his head down with the rein. This training is progressive in nature and will require some time to teach. Remember, with the gaited horse as the hind leg swings forward (in this case inside rear leg) the head goes down. The stretch is in the release. Using the concept that the stretch is in the release will carry into mounted work.

Some horses will be reluctant to drop their head because of prior training. This is because the poll, neck, and top line are tight with tension and stiffness. With this kind of horse, there is definitely built-in tension. It's been my experience across the board most horses are taught man-made braces caused by poor training. However some horses are born high-strung, which leads to built in braces without any man-made train-

126   From the Trail to the Rail

ing effects. What I call braces in horses are muscle groups that will not stretch and relax. With this type of horse you can teach dropping and stretching the head at the halt. Tack the horse in a halter and lead rope and stand facing the horse. Hold your left and right hands on the lead rope under the halter. You can, at the halt, put light downward pressure on the lead rope and ask for lowering or stretching of the head down. As soon as the horse's head goes down release the hold.

Now, with a rope halter under the bridle, lunge the horse over three or four ground poles eight feet apart. This will get your horse to drop his neck and head elevation. The main point is, don't get discouraged just stay working until the penny drops. Developing a long-term relaxation program for a better trail horse starts with getting the horse's head down and getting the top line relaxed to cure the pace. The gait is in the horse's top line. His heart and soul is in his mouth.

After a few minutes of groundwork with the horse already tacked up, you are ready to mount and ride. I recommend when re-training a horse that you use a round pen or other small riding enclosure. The reason for riding in a small area is to give the horse a chance to learn to stop in a snaffle bit.

One of the biggest problems with owners going from a shank to a snaffle bit is the horse may not want to stop and can run off with you. At trail riding facilities I remove shank bits from most horse's mouths in order to calm the horse's mind. The effects are immediate and most horses show a calming mind. The problem comes in when the horse flashes back with the riders on the trail. The horse runs off with them because he does not know how to stop. A snaffle bit is a tool and nothing more. The snaffle bit is used to communicate to all four corners of the horse's feet. I think a shank bit communicates only to the two hind feet. The horse has to be placed in a safe environment until he understands how a snaffle bit works.

Developing a one-rein stop is the first order of business in a safe round pen or other small enclosure. In the round pen if he runs off he's not going anywhere so just enjoy the ride.

It's at this point and time you may find the horse does not want to stand still when you mount. If you can't get on and off safely your chances of getting hurt have just doubled. This is a very common problem with shotgun-trained horses. This is one part of basic training that has to be taught with no gray areas. Just be firm and start working on the ground with the attitude the horse will stand still to mount. The horse will pick up on your attitude.

I like to present the horse with two options, either stand still when mounting, or go to work on the lunge line. Tack the horse up for riding using a rope halter underneath the bridle and attach a 15-foot lunge line to the halter. I would recommend a safe place to work. A small enclosure would be ideal.

If all the aforementioned groundwork for a calm mind has been accomplished, there should be little problem teaching your horse to stand still. Stand beside the left side of the horse and attempt to place your left foot in the stirrup. If he takes off or bolts forward make him go to work. Never mount a horse that is moving forward. Just step back on the ground and put him to work. Now here is where you attitude comes into play to get the job done! There is no room for misguided sympathy.

Work the horse on the lunge line for about five minutes then offer him a chance to stand still again. You're going to repeat this procedure until a change of behavior occurs and the horse stands still. The procedure outlined here may take up to five hours or longer when re-training a horse. More than likely you will see sweat dripping from under the girth.

The best policy is to not let this behavior get started in the beginning of the horse's training, but more times than not this behavior has been taught somewhere else. You have to correct the problem with time and patience. It's not about, "I'll show you horse who's boss." It's about you being persistent and consistent in getting the job done. Pet the horse and remember you're dealing with re-training problems. Be kind in your approach but get the job done for a safe trail mount in the future. A horse that will stand still is a good indicator of good ground work.

I use a different approach when just starting a young horse. Stand

 beside the horse's left side and attempt to place your left foot in the stirrup. If he takes off, or bolts forward turn him sharply around to face you. When I say the word sharply, I mean sharply. Go to the off side and stand him up sharply again and I mean sharply. If you don't have the strength, get a friend to act as the header and hold the lunge rope to stand the horse up and face the header. I use a similar process when teaching the horse's first ride in chapter 6. I spend a lot

From the Trail to the Rail

of time here with a young horse. Just one word of caution, if you cannot mount a horse with one fluid easy movement don't cause more problems because of your inability or physical condition to mount the horse. Get some help. For safety reasons I cannot overstate mounting and dismount training. I believe teaching a horse to use a mounting block is good horse sense.

Tack the horse with a snaffle bit and good fitting saddle. The goal is to develop the top line under saddle to cure the pace. Remember, "The higher the head the less brains, the lower the head the more brains." Burn this into your memory. I recommend a round pen or small enclosure. Mount the horse and ask for nothing. Determine his base line behavior. Ask yourself some questions: Does his head pop up like a goose? Does he speed off? Will he slow down? Is his back hollow? Is he pacing under saddle? Try and determine if the horse will calm and drop his head after five or ten minutes of riding. If the horse does, this is a short cut you can take full advantage of when re-training. Ride the horse and try to understand his point of view. Determining where he is mentally will give you a road map inside the horse's body to help correct the pace.

After a few rides start teaching the one-rein stop. Pick up the inside rein and hold. Bring your inside leg back and roll the inside hind leg over the outside hind leg. Notice if the horse stops, drop the contact with the inside rein, and let the horse rest. If the horse wants to keep rolling over the hindquarters just hold the rein until he stops moving. You sometimes get a horse that rolls over the hindquarters then starts off again without stopping. Just repeat until you get the one rein stop taught at 100% with no gray areas. Teaching the one rein stop will help teach the horse to separate his feet into an even four-beat gait. It is also a great exercise to introduce the calm-down cue.

When teaching the drop down cue (calm down cue) take up light contact with the reins. Start walking the horses on a small circle to the left. When you feel the left inside hind leg swing forward drop the contact with the inside rein first and follow the horse's head down with your arms with no rein contact. When you drop the contact and reach forward with your arms the horse's head and neck are already going down. Don't lean forward in the seat, just relax and let your arms forward with no contact is all it takes. You are just building on the natural movement of the horse. This will be different later when you stretch down into contact. Keep the work slow and steady with no force. You want the horse to think it's his idea to drop his head. It's amazing to watch a re-trained horse that drops his head and gets the feeling of relaxation. Letting him know it's ok to relax under saddle is what it's all about. This whole process will develop into a self-seeking reflex action for the benefit of the horse and rider. The horse wants to please by nature and it starts with us giving him an opportunity to relax under saddle. Relaxation of the back is a key ingredient for curing the pace.

Bear in mind, don't get in a hurry. Re-training a horse takes more time than starting a new horse. I believe for every hour the horse was ridden wrong it takes a week to correct that one hour. I have committed up to three to four years with some horses with great results. Sadly there were some that were too far over the edge to help, and a few that were just plain rogues. Now these horses are rare but you need to be told the truth of the matter, rogue horses are out there and they will hurt you if you're not careful.

There is nothing wrong with going into a holding pattern with the one-rein stop and the calm-down cue. Just spend a lot of time giving the horse time to adjust to the request on both reins. Let the horse follow his nose and neck stretched out towards the bit and down. Use this time to show your horse to the ground.

Use a good stand up seat with the seat bones lightly touching the saddle, yet with enough contact to influence and follow the motion of the horse's back. Determine how much of a request it takes or under what circumstances the horse pops up his head and hollows out his back. Observe the horse's behavior for answers to solving the pace. By now you should realize the key point is to rid the top line of stiffness and tension and getting the horse to stretch out and down. A good top line is the cure for the pace. The remainder of this chapter is exercises to help develop the top line properly to cure the pace.

The push and pull of muscle groups working together on each side of the horse's body takes several months to develop in the top line. Consider time as a long-term commitment without any thought of getting in a hurry. These exercises will also let you feel what a square horse is doing under saddle.

Riding over ground poles is a great way to get the horse to drop his head and lift his back. Tack the horse with a snaffle bit and saddle, place four ground poles on the ground about 15 feet apart in the round pen or other small enclosure. Place a pole at 12 o'clock, 6 o'clock, 9 o'clock, and 3 o'clock. You have already worked this pattern on the ground. The difference now is you have your weight on the horse's back. Ride the horse slowly on a loose rein to ensure he doesn't trip over the poles. Use

the light seat as described earlier. Keep light contact with reins and let the horse have his head to balance his movements. Keep the speed slow and let the horse step over the poles, not jump. Most horses will lower the head after a few minutes

From the Trail to the Rail

of work. Actively observe for the horse to lower his head and reward the horse with a kind word. Keep the horse bent on the circle, just being able to see his inside eye. Feel the square even gait for a few strides between each pole. Keep in mind this is what you are trying to achieve under saddle on flat ground. Don't overdo this exercise. It is very strenuous for the horse. At first about three or four times a week is fine.

Don't wrap yourself around the axles thinking you are creating a two-beat trot. The horse will revert back to pacing after a few minutes on a straight line. He does not have enough strength in his top line to keep walking. I have yet to see this exercise create high hock action in a horse. Believe it or not, with horses that have too much high hock action at the start this actually improves the hock action. The horse will start driving with his hocks with no wasted up and down hock motion. Keep in mind, you could use some trot now to help square up the horse. Ride slow and give the horse plenty of time to lift his back and separate his feet.

Hill work is my cup of tea. Hills are the quickest way to square up your horse. Not only will they help develop the top line but greatly assist in strengthening the hindquarters. What happens when a horse is pushing and stepping under his body is he is slightly rounding his back. Start using hill work only after you can handle the horse with a one-rein stop and have developed the calm-down cue. At the base of the hill ride up the hill slowly with a light stand up seat. Place your hands about shoulder width apart. Keep light contact with the horse's mouth. Ask the horse to walk slowly up the hill and feel the horse square up under you. Remain steady and slow and feel the square gait. Realize the gait is the result of the back lifting to a level top line. You will feel the four feet moving evenly, head nod, and overstride.

At the top of the hill let the horse stop, rest, and think about what he has just done. Be proud of him and show tons and tons of praise. He will pick up on your enthusiasm and will try to please you again in the future. Let the horse dog walk back down slowly. As he goes down the hill keep him slow and drop all contact in the mouth. If you go slow back down the hill he will definitely continue separating his feet.

At the base of the hill this time ask for a calm-down cue with no rein pressure. With the head and neck stretched down ask him to walk up the hill. Some horses, when reaching for the bit, will almost trot a few strides. When you get to top of the hill let the horse stop, rest, and think. If you want to dog walk back down the hill keep the horse's head elevation slightly up with light contact in the mouth. Be careful, too high a head will hollow the top line into a pace or stepping pace, especially going downhill.

When you get back to bottom of the hill let the horse stop, rest, and think about what he has done. At the base of hill this time let the horse walk up the hill with soft contact. This time at the top of the hill don't stop, let the horse turn and see how far he can walk along the crest of the hill before falling onto his forehand. You will soon begin to realize when he is walking off the hindquarters and not on the forehand. This is powerful piece of information to have in the seat of your pants. In my point of view when you horse is in good condition you cannot do enough hill work with plain flat walking.

Tall grass or straw about 18 inches deep is a good squaring tool. Find a field with tall grass or let your front yard grow up into a hay field. Riding the horse into the tall grass or 18 inch deep straw requires him to lift his front end higher. Please remember this, the horse lifts his front feet higher and lighter as a result of proper impulsion coming from the hindquarters.

Try this exercise. With your hands about shoulder width apart and light contact ride through the grass or 18 inches of straw. When you come out of that footing drop the contact and see if the horse drops his head into an ordinary walk or dog walk. If he does you are on the right track with re-training. Pat yourself on the back. You are now training a horse.

Riding in tall grass, straw, and on hills is only a band-aid to help in the cure. I have yet to find a tall patch of grass in a show ring. You have to keep working for a square gait getting the top line developed into transitions. The gait has to become the horse's idea.

It very important that the horse stretches out and down towards the bit. This concept will elude many seasoned trainers. The horse will do self-seeking reflex action with proper initial training but when you

are re-training you have to be very observant for the horse to understand what you want and capitalize on the movement when he gives it to you. There are a lot of names attached to working a horse that stretches out and down towards the bit. My spin is called a self-seeking reflex action. Just to name a few more: Neck reaching out, calm-down cue, neck stretching, reaching for the bit, drop down cue, working deep, and the list goes on and on. I'll go out on a limb and include the practice of dog walking. Teaching a horse to reach out and down is an essential teaching tool to cure the pace. The self-seeking reflex action must become a part of your horse's lifestyle. For teaching purposes I use so many different definitions because I have to say the same thing over and over again with different words. I don't think the equine world is going to change any time soon with a vast array of definitions with so many different words meaning the same connotations and denotations.

Everybody needs a place to go for relaxation. Some people take vacations, some take medication, and some abuse medications looking for a relaxed mind. A horse is no different. He needs a place to go for his mind and top line to become relaxed. Teaching him to stretch his head out and down is a natural endorphin release for a majority of horses. When a horse is picking grass he is relaxed. The moment his head goes up he is ready to flee or fight, depending on the situation. If the horse is ridden in a state of high tension with the head up like a goose he becomes fractious or an air head with time. He is never given the chance to relax and let his feet down.

The good news here is if you have been following the training intent outlined in this book you are already teaching this concept of stretching out and down. Then it becomes a self-seeking reflex action on the part of the horse.

Start walking the horse on a small circle to the left. Now when you feel the left inside hind leg swing forward drop the contact with the inside rein first and follow the horse's head down with your arms with no rein contact. When you drop the contact the head and neck are already going down and you are just building on the natural movement of the horse. This is good training for all gaited horses. Just ride the horse with complete slack in the reins for a reward.

Don't become discouraged with this concept in re-training a horse that has been shotgunned in his training, especially if he is nervous and flighty. It's going to take time for him to understand you are not going to hurt him in the mouth with the bit. If you break this training down on the mental side it's all about getting the horse to develop confidence in you and the bit. To get a horse's head down is no problem with a conditioned release, meaning you are rewarding for a right response. Problems creep in when you hang a piece of metal in the horse's mouth and ask him to trust humans who have already hurt him in the mouth. Horses don't forget but most will forgive.

Now getting the horse to reach down and stretch into contact is no big deal. As before, start walking the horses on a small circle to the left. This time, when you feel the left inside hind leg swing forward, drop the contact with the inside rein and follow the horse's head stretching down and out using your outside (right) rein. Keep a light contact with the right rein and never pull on the horse's face. When you drop the contact the head and neck are already going down, just maintain light contact and follow the natural movement of the horse. The purpose with this exercise is to teach the horse to accept contact. Also this exercise helps connect the hindquarters to the mouth. The horse's hindquarter energy travels over the top line to the mouth and recycles back to the hindquarters creating a circle of energy.

Using a half halt and squeezing an abused horse may cause the horse to flash back and run through the bit with too much speed. Knowing the horse and how much leg you can use at this point and time is wise training consideration. It's been my experience with a re-train horse you just have to think in your mind about using your legs and most re-train horses will respond by going forward immediately. As the re-training evens out you can start using half halts to get a more level and rounded frame. A keynote and important reminder, pulling on the horse's face will never accomplish anything in any teaching or curing the pace.

Keep in mind, you can use a half halt with horses that accept the leg without blowing up. I like to get a good half halt going into a curve and coming out of the curve. The half halt will help teach the horse to use his hindquarters and raise his back level. Just remember when teaching the half halt to use seat, legs, hands, in that order. A little push with the seat, squeeze with the legs, then catch the energy in your hands. Make sure you release into gait. The half halt durations should not last more than three to four seconds. The half halt will unlock many doors but don't at this point in time create more problems with an over-reaction. I highly recommend you only use your calves with no spurs. Eventually the horse will accept normal use of the leg with time and proper training.

Don't count the horse out when re-training. He has natural ability to separate our intentions on what we want, he just needs time to figure it out for himself. Within a couple of months he will learn the difference between a calm-down cue and stretching into contact cue. He will understand and start raising his back in half halt. Please remember, most horses want to please and will if given half a chance.

All horses are different and can do many different gaits at any given time. I like to look at the pace as not so much a problem but a tool we can use in the long run to help our horses achieve a good flat walk. I'm almost certain some of the methods outlined above will help cure the pace. One of the areas I like about the pace is it can be useful in teaching a horse to stride out (lengthen stride). Pacing a horse into a stepping pace and then squaring the horse in the mouth with the right amount of pressure is a World's Grand Champion show horse.

Task: Teach the horse to square from a pace into a flat walk (developed top line.)

Conditions: A slow walk in all types of terrain and under all weather conditions.

Standards: A good flat walk is a four-beat gait with an even footfall, the horse nods his head with an overstride.

Chapter Twentyfour: Problem Solving the Trot
Re-training on the Ground

"Bounce once if you believe in diagonal." Bumper sticker

The hard trot is a gait that does require a good seat to ride and appreciate. Many books have been written on how to ride the hard trot. The trot is a two-beat gait with the left front and right rear legs working together and the right front and left rear legs working in unison creating a two-beat gait with suspension. It is unlike the fox trot, which is a smooth four-beat gait. In the gaited horse world the hard trot is looked upon as a problem with the horse being too square and not smooth. The trot can become even more of a problem when you take your horse to a horse show and he trots around the ring. Most likely you have just wasted an entry fee.

The bounce in the hard trot can be very tough on your back, but don't forget the horse's back also takes a tremendous beating. One only has to look at early European history to find out royalty and people of high standing rode gaited horses. Everybody else had to figure out how to smooth out the hard trot. It didn't take long to figure out you needed a posting seat to follow the motion of the gait and save the horse's back. I think our greatest contribution in the equine world came from man's attempts to smooth out the common trotting horse. Today we have plenty of good easy gaiting horses across the world that excel in all areas of the equine industry.

In my opinion the horse that comes out of the flat walk and drifts toward a trot is a much easier problem to solve than a horse who is confirmed in the pace. Most of my time is still spent solving the pace, not the trot. I don't look at the trot as a faulty gait in the trail world. The trot will always be judged as a faulty gait in the show ring. Most gaited horses trot on the lunge line when working on a circle. When you see this behavior don't panic. The majority of horses will change just as soon as you add weight on their back.

Now don't be fooled with the popular notion of squaring only pacing horses for the show ring. You can find a show gait using the trot as a tool to develop a good flat walk into a finished show gait. I do treat the trot as a symptom you have to cure but not to the degree that I do with a pace bred horse.

I do not advocate raising the horse's head and hollowing the back to find some pace in the horse's gait. This method does work on a large percentage of horses but I find it does take a higher degree of riding experience to find the swing pace and not create more problems than you can solve, such as the horse losing his brains because his head is too high. If you are not careful you will go too far in the wrong direction.

For the horse that drifts toward the trot when adding speed you have to consider strengthening the hindquarters. You should be aware, a lot of horses will trot under saddle for a three or four-week period then switch over to a stepping pace. I believe the reason for this is when the horse is legged up and in shape he starts to carry you with different balance positions in his body. I have had some square going horses that experiment with balance points and find out on their own how to carry you. Just make sure you have a good understanding of what gait the horse is inclined to do and drifting towards.

I don't worry with too much shoeing or adding weigh to the hind feet. Riding barefooted on the front feet is fine for now. Leaving the hind feet bare footed is also fine for the first sixty days. After this period shoeing for a good balanced foot and a light toe weight shoe in the rear may help the trot gait.

The top line with the trotting horse has to be considered, just like with the pacing horse. Most of the time stiffness and tension results in a tight tail-bobbing lick. The hindquarters take short steps. The square-going horse can have a high head and hollow back to the same degree you see with a pacing horse and still be just as square. A horse that carries his back in an arched position will change the level of his back within a couple of weeks of riding, depending on where the rider is seated. I recommend a good old stand up seat or the cowboy seat as described in chapter 23 to help get the horse to swing.

A square-going horse that has been trained with shotgun methods to include mechanical training or hand-dominated riding will have tension in the top line and blow a fuse mentally just as quick as any other horse. There is no difference with a square going horse or any other type of gaited horse. The same slow and patient training has to be considered in developing the top line to carry a rider. You have to let the horse's natural ability unfold. You do this in a simple of way of just letting it happen slowly.

A good sound trainer will never cull a good square going horse for he knows that once the horse is trained this type of horse will stay trained. Some trainers will debate that a square going horse takes longer to train. My experience has been there is no difference in training time between a trotting gait and a pacing gait. Both horse are the same in the set period and bring similar mental problems in re-training.

Keep in mind you can get a combination of both trot and pace. It's been my experience that when a horse starts mixing and matching gaits this is usually created by man-made confusion. Horses become confused trying to figure you out and what you want. Look much deeper into your horse than a nice ride in the park. He wants to please you to the point of mental confusion. In my opinion, the only logical explanation for mixing and matching gaits is the horse is trying very hard to please his owner and the owner does not recognize the efforts on the part of the horse.

Bitting a square going horse is not a different procedure than I've defined with pacing horses. I use a good tongue relief snaffle bit or a combination bit. I've met a lot of old time trail trainers who are great at getting the right bit in a horse's mouth. Most of them will tell you it takes a certain amount of bit pressure to square up a horse into gait and this is true with a lot of horses. Now don't forget, this pressure is only the weight of two strawberries in each hand. I like using a bit that assists in getting the horse to reach forward and down, stretching into contact as defined in the last chapter. To say again, the stretch is in the release for self-seeking reflex action. The end result is you want to be able to release into gait.

I look at the trotting horse as an opportunity to let the top line develop into a square going horse. The reason I lean towards this direction is if you look at some earlier breeds, especially Tennessee Walking Horses in the western part of the country, Missouri Fox Trotters in the Ozark Mountain range, and the Rocky Mountain Horses in the Appalachian Mountain range, you find a smooth, square going horse that did not have to have gait modification. The old bloodlines that I'm referring to did not require gait modification in the top line that we see today in the show world. The popular style of horse today has been bred much more for pace than trot. I'll go out on a limb here and say the breeders have a long road to recovery.

In my opinion, there is nothing wrong with the ideal of having horses that you let off for the winter and start back in the spring that present no gaiting problems. As a matter of fact, this is the type of horse you need in harsher areas of winter where most owners don't have an opportunity to ride even if they wanted to enjoy a good trail ride. It seems to me we have to consider a square going type of horse with a good flat walk to fit the overall needs of modern trail riders.

When training a horse or re-training a horse there is no reason to try to re-invent the wheel, if it works, it works. Please refer to chapters 4 through 9, 21, and 22 for training and re-training a horse to develop trust and a calm mind. There is no difference in this training for the square going horse.

The reason the groundwork does not change with the square going horse is that collecting the mind before collecting the body is a great way to square up a trotting horse. The words pain, fear, excitability, and muscle tone mean the same thing for a square going horse as a pacing horse. As riders and trainers we cannot make different concepts to fit a different moving horse. No matter what breed of horse you decide to ride the horse can and will get high-headed and hollow-backed in the top line with poor riding. Getting the horse calm and relaxed on the ground puts you well on your way to having a great trail horse under saddle.

Task: Teach the horse to square from a trot into a flat walk (developed top line).

Conditions: A slow walk in all types of terrain and under all weather conditions.

Standards: A good flat walk is a four-beat gait with an even footfall, and the horse nods his head with an overstride.

Chapter Twentyfive: Problem Solving
the Trot Under Saddle

"You cannot train a horse with shouts and expect it to obey a whisper."
Dagobert D. Runes

When training or re-training a too square horse I recommend two schools of thought. The first method I like is to ride in a dog walk doing nothing but building a gearbox into a flat walk. This is where the old time saying originated, "all you have to do is put on a bridle and ride." The second method is to teach the horse to swing without creating a high-headed hollow-backed horse.

If you try to use a shank bit to solve problems you can get an over-reaction caused by pain in the horse's mouth. It does not take very many overreactions to create mouth tension and develop all sorts of behavioral problems. I see this time and time again with horses showing signs of resistance on the trail or the rail. You must have good soft contact with your hands to calm the horse's mind. Soft contact starts with a good bit that offers tongue relief and solves many training or re-training problems. Usually an older horse's mind will calm quickly when there is no bit pain. If you get a calm mind by changing to a bit with tongue relief you will definitely get a short cut in re-training. With this in mind I always look at the mouth first for potential problems.

When training the trotting horse, tack the horse with a mild snaffle tongue relief bit and a good saddle fit. As before, your horse needs to understand groundwork for a calm mind, know how to follow his nose, turning, stopping, mounting and dismounting. Please refer back to chapters 1 through 6. I consider the aforementioned areas basic horse training. These training matters should be resolved prior to modifying the trot into a flat walk. Getting the horse to understand the rear-end under, front-end across, one-rein stop, calm-down cue, reaching down and fore-ward are the same precursors as with the pacing horse. The procedures outlined in chapter 23 for stretching into contact and releasing into gait are the same training and re-training as stated before. The only difference now is the movement is a two-beat trot.

Start the horse out in a dog walk with the horse's head down just out from his withers. Let the horse find his natural head carriage. Walk the horse on a loose rein, just getting him to separate his feet. Don't get in a hurry. It's going to take several months to build strength in the hindquarters. A good attitude to have is to take the time it takes. Just remember, if your horse does

not square in several months then it's going to take several more months. Just keep working towards your goal. You just have to believe in yourself and be patient. If you start to shake in confidence just believe in your horse. He will square more times than not into a sharp gaited horse.

Several years ago I had a group of horses in re-training. Several of the horses came from commercial training barns. Most of the horses were culled because they were too square (trotting). Two of the horses did not square as fast as I liked. Now as luck would have it I had the time to ride the horses with my schedule. All I did was just dog walk both horses on the trail. The truth of matter was I was at my wit's end with their trotting movements. Now both horses could walk on loose rein in dog walk with the best of horses with soft contact in a snaffle bit, but with a hint of speed both horses were confirmed in the trot. I thought to myself, "at least we can be the best dog walking horses in the world," and that's all we did was dog walk. We dog walked slowly for several more months until I figured out that riding both horses slowly had caused both horses to loosen up and swing into a flat walk.

Too many horses are culled in the belief the horses are too square. Just give the square going horse more time to strengthen his hindquarters and loosen his top line. I have seen a square going horse, more times than not, when trained, have a better front end and hindquarters for the show world. I can say this without being too critical. A lot of commercial horse training barns have given away a small fortune in the belief that the horse is too square. The norm is, instead of taking the time to train the square going horse they cull the horse.

I have had some luck in training a square going horse to swing pace and then square back up into a flat walk. I like working a horse down a hill in order to get his feet moving more lateral, then square back into a flat walk. The theory is from a trot you teach a stepping pace going to the other side of the scale and move back towards the flat walk. The only downfall with this training is some horses can start pacing. A horse that requires more hindquarter maintenance falls into this category.

Find a mild sloping hill with good footing. Use a snaffle bit with no curb chain. Let the horse find his own head elevation, give a half halt and ride down the hill a few times getting the horse used to the new demands. Notice the base line behavior and what gait the horse is doing going down the hill. If he is giving you a stepping pace leave him alone and just keep working with him going doing down the hill in stepping pace. Walk back up the hill in a flat walk.

Now if he is trotting down the hill use a stand up seat. As the front left leg leaves the ground weight, the left side of the horse's body. When the right front leaves the ground, weight the right side of the horse's body. With light contact squeeze your hand each side of the horse's mouth in coordination with your feet. Do not pull on the horse's mouth.

Alternate squeezing with your hand and leg on the same side acting together just with this concept in mind for a couple lessons (20 minutes) and see if the horse start finding your rhythm of a stepping pace. After a couple of lessons if the horse is still trotting don't panic, he will change into a stepping pace.

I've seen many Quarter Horses learn to fox trot doing what I call "the rock". Using a good stand up seat, ride down the grade but this time rock (shift) your weight side to side in the saddle. When I say rock your weight I mean rock your weight to point of displacement. Displacement of your weight causes your horse to catch your weight on alternating sides as he steps forward, making it very difficult for him not to stepping pace. I have found this very effective in getting a horse to pace. Just work up slowly to this point. More times than not you can get your horse to stepping pace. Bear in mind you don't want to go too far in the wrong direction, especially if you get the head too high and hollow the back.

After several twenty minute lessons the horse will stepping pace when asked to on flat ground. Don't forget to ask yourself a question: "I got him pacing, now what should I do?" The answer is to use the stepping pace to loosen the horse up into a flat walk. The stepping pace is only a tool to assist you in getting the horse's top line and hindquarters developed. This gait can turn into confusion if the utmost care is not taken. I comment on this matter because it's a tool that can help loosen some horses. I do find square going horses that loosen up in the top line square up nicely and go into the flat walk in a sporty manner.

When you find the gait you want don't stick on the reins with the horse, give him a release into gait. I like to use the release into gait with the desired gait or the finished gait. The release has to mean something to the horse. If the release means nothing to the feet it will be hard for the horse to separate your intentions. This is why I don't like to take hold of a horse and teach him to pace off bit pressure. I feel it causes way too much confusion. I use only soft contact to keep tension out of the mouth and top line. All this will help with a release into self-carriage in later training.

Teaching a horse to stepping pace with light contact lets him find out what his feet are doing. He thinks it's his idea and that's ok. You want your horse to do your thing his way and like doing his job. Just stay out of the way and let it happen with soft contact. You hear a lot of people say to ride the horse out of his mouth. Again this is somewhat misleading. Does it mean put pressure in the mouth with pull? Or does it mean let the reins flop on the horse's neck? I can only say what it means to me is to keep enough pressure on the horse's mouth to keep the reins from flopping and not stick on the reins. You always look for an opportunity to release into a gait into the flat walk. When you feel the gait just give an additional release with the fingers and the horse will know he's done right.

I have gotten some good results with a square going horse that does not hang in the trotting gait. This type of horse moves out of the flat walk when speed is added into a trot. Then when you add more speed the horse goes into a stepping pace. Pay attention to your horse and play with the horse and see how his feet naturally want move. Take advantage of anything he gives you to help develop a good top line.

I add a quick burst of speed only with soft contact using my calves, no spurs. Some horses jump into a flat walk, fox trot, running walk, or pace. You just have to be observant and see what you're holding. If you have a re-training situation be careful with over-use of the leg with a high-head-ed, hollow-backed horse in order not to cause an overreaction. If you keep this type of horse keyed up it will be harder for him to relax into any gait. Top line tension will result in a tail-bobbing lick disconnected from the hindquarters.

I do use (cavaletti) ground poles for the square going type of horse. Again don't fall into the trap of thinking that ground poles make a gaited horse into a two-beat trotting horse. This is mutated thinking when training horses. Hopefully by now you are beginning to understand the gait is in the horse's top line. The ground poles help develop the top line, hocks and get the head down for a good stretch into gait.

Ground poles are demanding exercise don't overtax the horse, about three or four times a week working up to 15 to 20 minute lessons, with dwell (stop) time. Place four poles about 15 feet apart in a small round pen or other small 25 foot by 25 foot enclosure. I use a 22-foot lunge rope. Using the clock method, place one pole at 12 o'clock, one at 6 o'clock, one at 3 o'clock, and one at 9 o'clock. Remember to ride the horse in a walk over the ground poles. He will slow down and sometimes even stop to look and lower his head. When you see the horse start to drop his head this is the time to reward and take pressure off the horse's face. If he starts to rush slow him with alternating pressure on each side of his mouth.

Most square going horses will come to gait with just good disciplined riding. Now what I mean is, do you have enough discipline to work in a dog walk for a flat walk and not ask for anything else? Keep the show lick out of your head at this point and time. When you get the gait you want, release into gait for reward. Let rest be long in the work. Let the horse stop, rest, and think about what he is doing. Riding on the trails is a great way to square up trotting horses into gait.

One of the things in re-training or solving gait problems is not to push the horse too hard. Watch his breathing. Don't push into exhaustion and teach the horse how to quit by getting things overdone. When you get the desired result, praise your horse and stop for the day. Always stop on a good note and you will start on a good note at the next lesson. I have gone back and forth in solving gait problems because the horse can do so many different gaits that need attention. If you work the horse slowly and take your time many problems will disappear. Remember, the horse goes as you ride him.

Task: Teach the horse to square from a trot into a flat walk (developed top line).

Conditions: A slow walk in all types of terrain and under all weather conditions.

Standards: A good flat walk is a four-beat gait with an even footfall, the horse nods his head with an overstride.

Chapter Twentysix: The Canter

"A canter is a cure for all evil." Benjamin Disraeli

There is common myth in the gaited world that you don't canter young gaited horses. I don't know who started this line of thinking but the truth of the matter is you should start teaching the canter on the natural canter side. Now what I mean by the natural canter side is, which side does the horse take the canter lead naturally? A good place to find out the answer is watching the horse at liberty in the field. He will tell you. Just when I think the right side is the favorite side across the board I'll get a string of horses that like the left side. Just be observant and watch which lead he likes to take at liberty and teach that side first.

I like teaching the canter because it helps break the shoulders loose and improves the horse's reach. The shoulder roll is pretty to watch and is an extension of the shoulder not only in the canter but also in the flat walk. The canter helps built impulsion and gives you a correct feel of impulsion from the hindquarters. I would caution you to ensure your horse has been legged up with enough strength and balance to carry you safely.

Too much difficulty is made out the canter. It's a very easy gait to understand and develop. Don't make it into something tough to teach. The hard part in teaching the canter is for the owner first and foremost to understand the gait. Once you get the feel in the seat of your pants it becomes very easy to teach. Try to spend some time riding a good horse that is easy to canter. Feel the motion inside your body. For the most part, having the motion inside your body is all you need to teach the canter.

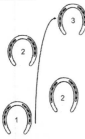

I teach riders and horses to canter most of the time on the right lead in a three-day clinic. This is not because I'm smarter or have some secret that teaches the canter. I recognize when the rider and horse team have enough balance to work together to achieve the canter. With that in mind it's very easy to teach the canter. I put the rider and horse in a balanced position that requires a three-beat rhythm (gait) on the correct lead, using a 'J'–turn, to the right on a hill.

Right Lead Canter

The canter is a three beat gait, 1-2-3, 1-2-3, 1-2-3. I think it would be fair to say the canter is a refined gallop slowed down into a definite three-beat gait. One must understand which is the leading leg before you start teaching the canter. The leading leg is the foreleg leading farthest out in the direction you're traveling. For instance, you're traveling to the right. The leading leg would be the right front leg. A reasonable explanation is when going in this direction of travel this is the safest way a horse can use his feet.

Left Lead Canter

From the Trail to the Rail

By nature the left leg traveling in the lead on a right circle could trip the horse or break a leg with a fall. When you walk a circle to the right you don't like to cross your left leg in front or behind the right leg on a circle and neither does your horse. Now don't get confused with counter canter at this time, which is beyond the scope of this book. I do think it is important that the horse knows which lead the rider wants to work and uses the correct lead.

When first teaching the canter, letting him use his natural lead is ok. Remember, you want to develop both sides of his body into straightness. When you break the right lead canter down into steps the first beat is the starter beat, left outside hind. The second beat is (simultaneously) left front and right rear (acting as one beat) and the third beat is the right front (lead). A lot of times when we ride finished horses we tend to forget that it took time to teach the canter.

Western pleasure horses are wired to lope. Just keep adding speed and you will get a lope (canter). The key point with a gaited horse is when he is supple the canter becomes very easy. Have you ever wondered why the canter is taught at the end of books?

There are as many ways to cue a horse to canter as there are bits. I had a friend that could reach up with his right hand, take his hat off and the horse would go into a right lead canter. He would get a big kick out of this trick and show how to use his left hand removing the hat and get left lead canter. Now when you rode this horse you could take your hat off all day long and not get a canter. What he was not telling his audience was that the cue came from his seat.

The procedures listed below are what have worked best for me over the years and most certainly are not the only way to teach a canter. More and more owners are teaching horses to canter on the lunge line and with very good results. However the rules change when you add weight on the horse's back. The lunge line can be effective when praising the horse and creating a good bridging word. I like to use the word "canter" as a bridging word. Working on the lunge I say the word "canter" and then place pressure on the hip and start the horse cantering. You keep work-

ing with the word "canter" until the horse understands and associates the word with desired movement (canter). The idea is when you start under saddle you repeat the bridging word "canter" the horse will canter.

This can be effective if properly presented with treats as a motivator. Just like my friend who cued the horse with the

seat bone built a bridging cue with the hat being taken off with the hand. If another rider could duplicate my friend's seat bone cue the horse would respond with the same canter.

Tack your horse with snaffle bit and a good fitting saddle. I would highly recommend the horse be supple and confirmed in the flat walk. Set up a course with one traffic cone at the bottom of a gentle hill. It does not have to be a traffic cone, anything to ride around will do just fine. Use the hill as a tool to develop the top line and work into gait. Ride to the bottom of hill and around the traffic cone. Make sure your turn is a shallow, small turn to the right around the traffic cone. As the inside hind leg steps deep under the horse's body squeeze with both legs, hold contact with the right hand as the leading rein. Use the outside left hand to regulate the bend. Your outside left leg can then slide behind the girth to start the canter. The horse will step into a right lead canter. The horse will go about three or four strides and fall onto the forehand. Praise the horse, go back to a walk and start over. Some horses don't try very hard so you don't know when to ask for more and when to back off. I'm satisfied when at first I get three or four good strides and then build on the effort.

I like to teach the horse to use his feet in an upward transition first, then let his balance run its natural course. Using the hill you can get his feet in the right place to strike off with the canter. Get the feet in right position, teach the cue first and then let him find his balance on his own time as you ride. Once he knows and understands what you want the hill will help him stay in balance and let him carry you longer in the canter.

What your horse did before he did the first bit of canter is powerful piece of information if you will take time to think about it and apply it as a concept for getting the feet in the right position. Keep putting him in the same position for success. He will get consistent in a hurry.

One of the reasons I like to let the balance run a natural course is it can lead to other short cuts in training. Observe very closely what gait the horse does when he loses his balance in the canter. A lot of times he will give you a great downward transition into a flat walk. Letting him develop balance on his own teaches him not to canter up every hill he comes to on the trail.

Ride your horse on flat ground to the left on a 60-foot circle into smaller circles, spiraling in. As you feel the horse slow turn back to the right sharply. Make sure your turn to the right is a sharp turn around your inside right leg. As the horse's right hind leg steps deep under the horse's body squeeze with both legs, hold contact with the right hand as a leading rein. Use the outside left hand to regulate the bend. After the squeeze quickly slide the outside left leg behind the girth to start the canter. More times than not the squeeze is all you need from the legs. The horse will step into right lead canter. If your horse is too hot off the leg use a limited amount of a squeeze with the legs. Just thinking about a squeeze is enough to shift his balance into a canter.

Ride your horse on flat ground going into a curve clockwise. This time place weight on the right stirrup, bend the horse's head to the left side towards the rail just to see the left eye. Squeeze with both legs asking for the horse to catch his balance onto a right lead canter. Some trainers advocate using the left leg to push more or be more active in an attempt to displace the horse off balance so he falls into right lead canter.

No matter what canter cues you use to teach the horse to canter, I like to finish into systems that allow for upper level work.

I recommend the following finished canter aids to the right. Sit deeper on the left seat bone, press your left leg behind the girth to displace hindquarters in (haunches in). This will set up the outside hind leg for the strike off. Light contact with the right rein to bring the nose in to see the right eye. Outside left rein to regulate the amount of bend. When the horse gives you the canter, praise the horse, and release into gait.

Keep this in the back of your mind. The better legged up (conditioned) your horse is the easier it is to teach the canter. The good news is when he learns to carry weight on his back in the canter he will not forget. I think by now the answer to the question: Is the canter a natural rhythm for the gaited horse? is absolutely "yes". This is why the canter is so easy to teach.

Other disciplines have just as many problems with the canter as the gaited world. I teach the canter when I feel the horse has enough top line and balance to carry the rider. You have to decide how far you want to develop the canter. If you are subscribing to the show world you may want to take the canter very seriously, not only because it's a requirement but because it's a great gait to loosen the shoulders and teach impulsion, not speed. The canter will definitely help get the front end off the ground and light. Spending time teaching your horse to canter is a wise investment. A horse that canters on both leads is priced higher with the canter in mind.

After about six months of practice, the one canter exercise I like to teach is the simple lead change. Start riding your horse in a 60-foot figure-eight circle. This figure-eight is two circles side by side, not the traditional number eight. You can start on the right side circle going to the right in a flat walk. Walk the circle a few times getting the horse used to the demands. Using the right rein, make sure you can see the inside right eye. Use the left rein to regulate the bend. Keep the horse bent on the circle with the inside right leg active at the girth. Use your outside leg behind the girt to assist in keeping the bend. As you get to where the two circles touch go the other way in a flat walk.

This time you use the left rein to see the inside left eye and the right rein to help regulate bend. Use your left leg active at the girth and right leg slightly behind the girth to help regulate the bend. Ride the circle at a flat walk. After a few rounds, when you reach the spot where the circles touch, cue the horse into a canter. Hopefully by this time your cues are starting to be set in stone. Feel the horse go into the canter and ride for a few rounds in the canter. Prior to where the circles touch, about two strides away, drop back down into a flat walk. When the circles touch, cue the horse into a left canter lead. When you can ride this pattern you are well on your way in teaching a good sound-moving horse.

Most of the problems I see with the canter are that the gaited horse needs a good conditioning program. You will be amazed how quickly problems will disappear with proper conditioning and the help of a good professional trainer. The more serious problems are medical in nature and do require a good vet looking at the hindquarters, stifles, hocks, and top line.

Many gaited horse canter automatically on the lunge line but don't always under saddle. Some faults can be caused by rider problems in the seat. The rider's balance, timing, and leaning off to one side are areas I find at my clinic that needs the most corrections. A horse not taking the correct lead is nothing more than a teaching problem that will disappear with the right trainer. Getting impulsion right from the hindquarters, not speed, will develop any gaited horse into a fun trail or rail horse.

Tasks: Teach the horse to do a 3-beat canter on both leads when cued by the rider.

Conditions: After the horse has developed a good flat walk take advantage of gentle hills, 'J'–turns, and circles to introduce and teach the canter. Start with the lead the horse prefers naturally.

Standards: The canter is a three-beat gait, done in a calm manner at a moderate speed. The horse should take both leads using the following finished canter aids: Sit deeper on the outside seat bone, press your outside leg behind the girt to displace the hindquarters in haunches in. This will set up the outside hind leg for the strike off. Use light contact with the inside rein to bring the horse's nose in to see the inside eye. The outside rein regulates the amount of bend.

Chapter Twentyseven: Shoeing Considerations

"One can't shoe a running horse." Dutch Proverb

Years ago when I was just starting out training gaited horses, I realized a farrier could not nail a flat walk on a horse. It takes an equal amount of training and shoeing to make a quality horse. Finding a good gaited horse farrier in your area can be a hard challenge. With that in mind I wanted you to read a chapter on shoeing a gaited horse from a good friend of mine who has been shoeing horses for 30 years. Charlie Roach is not only a good farrier, he is also a well-respected natural horse clinician in his own right. His approach to shoeing and natural training in both areas has enhanced his working knowledge in the type of shoeing that will assist you and give you a road map to start learning about the shoeing needs of a gaited horse. I think you will find a balanced foot is what Charlie Roach is teaching not only to customers and students, but upcoming young trainers who are making a difference one horse at a time.

I'm not going to spend time arguing with you over using weight on your horse's feet. That is a personal note between you and your farrier. You are the one who eventually has to decide what's in the best interest for your horse and in keeping with your situation. My personal experience has been the lighter you can keep a horse's feet in the set period the better quality gait you will have when the horse matures. Each horse described in this book has certain rules that are promulgated within their respective show industries. A good place to start is looking at the trail divisions and your farrier for your horse's shoeing needs.

My favorite rules for training a horse also apply to shoeing a horse. The farrier can't get hurt, the horse can't be hurt, and the horse is calmer after the shoeing experience. One must understand it is the owner's responsibility to get the horse ready for shoeing, not the farrier's. The rest of this chapter is devoted to Charlie Roach's approach to shoeing the gaited horse.

By Charlie Roach

This chapter covers the trimming and shoeing of the pacey or trotty gaited horse regardless of breed. When it comes to the shoeing department all my ideas have been developed as a professional trainer of the Tennessee Walking Horse for over twenty years. My shoeing experience has been developed for over thirty years as a professional farrier for Rocky Mountain Horses, Missouri Fox Trotters, and Tennessee Walking Horses along with principles for all gaited and lateral moving horses.

The first thing a person must understand is whether or not their horse is pacey or trotty. After determining the type of horse you are dealing with you must next determine just how much the horse leans towards the pace or trot. You can use a scale as depicted below to help determine the horse's gait.

If a person is not sure where the particular horses falls on being pacey or trotty, seek out a knowledgeable person to help. The shoeing principles become non-effective without proper diagnosis. After determining the horse's gait, one must proceed in an attempt to change the balance, speed of the footfall, and arc of the limb, considering the horse's conformation.

Principles for shoeing the pacey horse:

What to do with the now declared pacing type of horse? First I would start by attempting to obtain a longer front foot. For example, on a 15-hand high horse I would strive towards a balanced 4" to 4½" inch toe. Keep in mind most Quarter Horses have a 3½" to 4" toe. I would ensure the horse's feet are level and land flat with each step, not rolling from an outer or inner edge onto the foot. Remember not to sacrifice strong, sturdy, healthy feet for length.

Secondly, I would go with a heavier front shoe, as this will slow the front end down. For example: A ⅜" x ¾" steel front shoe with caulks. If the horse is real pacey try a ½" x 1" steel shoe with caulks. Keep in mind, more weight on the front feet can cause the horse to labor pace, which is not desirable. Also bear in mind, heavier shoes or caulks may not be safe for the horse on some types of terrain.

When it comes to the angle of the front foot I would go with a natural angle basically following the slope of the shoulder and pastern area. On most horses dropping the hoof angle one obtains a higher arc. These principles must be experimented with to obtain the best results. Bear in mind that keeping a naturally balanced foot with conformation will yield good results in the long run with proper training. When changing angles change slowly over a 6-month period. Bear in mind that changing angles increases the risk of injury for a horse that is ridden on rocky, uneven, hard ground.

Principles for shoeing the pacey horse's rear feet:

First step: Trim the toes back as short as possible without causing him to be sore. Secondly, the angle of the rear foot on a pacing horse with too much stride should be higher in angle. A toe length of 3⅜" with rear angle of 55 degrees is typical.

The rear shoe on a pacing horse should be as light and short as possible with caulks. In extreme cases I have used an aluminum shoe with a toe grab and caulks. It would also serve the purpose in extreme cases to leave the rear shoes off, as long as it's not detrimental to the soundness of the rear feet.

Shoeing and trimming the trotting horse:

Let's begin with the front feet by obtaining as short a toe as possible. Example: On a 15-hand horse, a 3½" toe would be acceptable. The heel of the front foot on the trotting type horse should be high in angle. When measuring the heel do not confuse height with length. The heels of the front feet should sit upright to quicken the breakover and make it easier for the rear legs to swing under.

Front shoes should be as light as possible. An example of this would be ¼" thick x ½" wide without caulks. One might also look at the aluminum shoe for lightness if it's not practical to go barefoot in the front feet for a period of time. This too would enhance more action. The desired angle of the trotting horse's front feet is 55 degrees.

Moving to the rear feet of a trotting horse one would go with a longer rear toe. I don't personally like an excessively long toe. It seems to make the horse trip behind and gets in the way of their good lateral motion. Examples of the toe length of the rear feet of a 15-hand horse are 4" to 4¼". The type of shoe for the rear of a trotting horse would depend on the severity of the trot. I utilize anywhere from ⅜" x ¾" steel shoe without caulks to a ½" x 1" inch steel shoe without caulks. A diamond brand toe-weight shoe is helpful if one can put up with the nail pattern and the increased risk of injury when the horse is worked on hard, rocky, uneven ground.

I would like to express that a farrier can only alter the gait when the horse has been shod improperly to begin with. The change only comes from bringing the horse back to the normal balanced foot. Remember that if a horse is 40 percent too lateral or 40 percent too diagonal the shoeing within itself will not cure the entire gait. Although the horse that is properly shod will definitely enhance your success at obtaining a desirable gait, especially when you add natural techniques of natural horsemanship (discussed in other chapters).

Many different horse breeds advertise the natural smooth gaits that have made them so popular for pleasure riding. Although in the process of change from purpose to purpose (utility horse to show horse to trail horse) the popular show horses have altered the breeding lines to get a gait that fits the trends for the show world. I too, like the popular high stepping, fast moving show horses but without sacrifice of correctness of gait. Now remember, in the process of breeding we must determine the desired purpose of each horse. It appears to me that in many breeds owners have purchased a mount for trail purposes that was bred for show purposes. The show horse breeding has been done with much consideration of more "go" than "whoa". Now this is what we find with more "go" than "whoa," an extremely lateral movement that is not suitable for a leisurely trail riding horse.

Sometimes, through re-programming the horse, and altering shoeing practices, it is possible to "make" him into a pleasurable trail-riding mount. Re-programming is discussed in other chapters in this book.

In pursuit of our perfect, natural, smooth gaited horse only through careful breeding and considerations can we produce that perfect animal. In the meantime we will utilize natural horsemanship practices along with proper horseshoeing to obtain our desired temperament and gaits. I hope this information will provide knowledge for humans to more enjoy the perfect horse, which God has created and given us. *Charlie Roach*

Chapter Twentyeight: The Show Gait, Considerations and Judging

"Two words not commonly related to winning or losing at the horse show ring do correlate with the color of the ribbons received. The two words are act and react. Winners act. Non winners react." Don Burt

Have you ever wonder what is the difference between a trail horse and a show horse? Ask this question around Kentucky barns and you will get as many different answers as types of horses. I can only share with you what my spin is in developing a nice show horse. For the most part it all starts in going back to the start of this book and developing a good flat walk and then letting the horse find his finished gait. You stay out of the way and let the horse develop his athletic ability.

Anita Howe exhibiting her Tennessee Walking Horse stallion, Papa's Royal Delight (Papa Joe's Pride x RB's Delight).

There are a few leading indicators that you need to look for that I think make all the difference in the world. You can sure save yourself a lot of frustration if you can find the right type of horse. First and foremost, look for a horse that has talent and wants to walk in a sportier lick. He will present a picture of, "look at me" with style that is unique to his disposition. This type of horse is born with good hindquarters. The horse drives with his hocks with no wasted up and down motion, everything

From the Trail to the Rail   153

goes smooth and forward. He has natural ability to maintain his rhythm. His motion is counterbalanced in the flat walk with a good head nod. Believe it or not, barefooted, or the weight of a light-shod shoe makes little difference in his performance. The show horse has natural ability to reach out of the shoulder into the flat walk. The reach out of the shoulders and hindquarters are very defining characteristics and should be given a lot of thought when selecting a show horse. This type of horse is a very calm-minded horse at home and tends to come alive at horse shows but is never unruly. You will definitely feel him compete with other horses saying, "Look at me." You will see this type of horse holding a happy tail, just gently lifted with a slow swinging motion. Many trainers are looking every day for this type of horse.

I'm confirmed in the belief a good show horse understands our desire to show and he also likes to strut his stuff. The horse's mouth should feel like power steering on a car, there is no drag on the forehand. More times than not, this type of horse accepts the bit without any problems. I can't say which is better, a gelding, mare, or stallion. I've seen equal ability in all three. To me it really doesn't matter. The bottom-line is, if you own this type of horse, count your lucky stars. This type of horse will always be at the forefront of any class. Now I'm not saying you can't flat walk a horse into a great show gait. You can, but you will be hard pressed to outperform a super athletic horse that likes his job.

When first starting the show type of horse you will notice several of these characteristics under saddle very quickly in the training process. You need to realize the show type of horse has to be trained just like his trail cousins. When you get the above described talent, go slow with this horse. Take your time and have a long-range goal. Look for a good five-year-old show horse to carry you well into his golden years. Don't ask for a whole lot of gait at any one time, just let it develop and unfold like a summer rose. You can train a great show horse on the trail with nothing more than good flat walking. Bear in mind, a great show horse must know and understand a half halt. Spend hour after hour developing the half halt. It is the tool that gets the horse on his hindquarters and helps gets the front end light. Anything else, say hello to the Horse Protection Act.

Shoeing can help the show horse, but remember to keep the shoeing as light as possible for the horse to do his job. It is very wise idea to know show classifications and shoeing requirements. Each classification is different with different shoeing requirements.

As already stated, you develop the horse with a clear plan of tasks, conditions, and standards, using the classical training scale as a road map to success. Get the top line in shape to hold gait in a consistent flat walk. Getting the horse to stretch down and forward as a cue, teach the horse to stretch into contact. Teach a firm understanding in the horse's mind to release into gait. Pulling on your horse's face with snaffle bit or a shank bit will, in the long run, only serve to teach him to stay on the forehand, dulling his mouth. You want lightness in the shoulders coming from light contact in the mouth. What I'm trying to describe in this book is classical dressage, not modern dressage where you see rider after rider skiing in the poor creature's mouth with bit pressure all in the name of contact.

I don't advocate putting a young horse in a frame. I like to let him find his own natural head set while training in the set period. The head set is classically in line with his age of development. You most certainly raise the head elevation later with a good top line developed. Pulling on the horse's face, tie downs, and draw reins are quick fixes that just do not work in the long run for most horses. In my opinion, the show world will just have to take second seat to good, sound training and the development of the horse's mind and body. Remember, you have a lifetime of showing the horse starting at four years of age. Too many horses are spoiled between the age of two and three in search of unrealistic expectations for the show world. Try to avoid this land mine and stay with what is in the best interest of your horse. Keep developing your flat walk into a self-carriage, working gait using the hindquarters. You need to be aware that your horse's hocks are not developed until four of five years of age.

What makes a great trainer is his or her ability to know when to add pressure and keep the horse's mind calm. I see very little need to re-invent the wheel to train the show horse. The chapters outlined in this book will produce a good show horse and in some cases, world class show horses.

It's been my experience you need at least ten horse show evaluation periods under your belt with a young horse. There is nothing wrong with taking your three-year-old horses to a local show. Let them get used to the sights and sounds. I would recommend at the first few shows use a snaffle bit so as not to cause an overreaction if you have to correct the horse. Spend more time leading the horse than riding. This is a great way to introduce the horse to the show world. When the horse turns four start showing him at local shows. Don't expect too much at the first couple of shows, just let him have time to learn what is expected of him. You will get a good feel of the horse's ability and how he will place at future shows. Pay attention to the calm mind and how relaxed the horse is in a strenuous environment.

If everything is going good, you should see steady improvements at each show. Just go with the attitude to have fun and enjoy yourself. The evaluation period will give you time to determine what class your horse is best suited for: Western, or Trail Pleasure, or one of the more animated classes. You will have to make this call depending on his natural ability and how you have developed the show gait.

The show gait of any horse is an extension of your ability to train the horse to a higher standard. Look for talent in the horse and give him time to develop into a show horse. Keep in mind, not every horse for every trainer or every trainer for every horse. Some trainers are going to find the right combination where everything clicks and the horse comes into his own. When you get this type of training situation it makes for a great horse. The same horse with someone else may not get the same sterling results. The best advice I can give you is to train slowly, shoot for the stars using sound training principles. Be patient and see if the horse develops to the standard. Aim high. If he makes it half way to a high standard it's a very respectable goal.

Now this brings us to this point, training a horse for the show world can be a rewarding experience, or a mine field with an explosion every three feet. I think one must come to an understanding that showing a horse first and foremost must be fun. Always remember you are paying for the opinion of a person that does not know as much about the horse you have trained as you do. Showing a horse is an expensive way to be miserable, if not done in the correct spirit.

If a judge can't ride and train a horse to work naturally out of the hindquarters he or she will never be able to properly judge a horse show, even if they have been judging for a lifetime. Ask yourself a question: Who bears the greater responsibility at any horse show, the Owner, Trainer, HIO, or the Judge? In my opinion the Judge has an ethical responsibility to do the right thing in the face of enormous pressure. Making the right call is not always the popular outcome at a horse show. It only takes about five classes to understand where the judge's head is ethically and his ability to understand his role to tie a free going horse that is not sore.

Some judges go out on a limb to tie commercial training barns that will be judging next week. You hear a popular term, "Will he hook?" meaning, will he tie a horse for a percentage of a sale? An example: Commercial barn A, who is judging the local weekend horse show, calls commercial barn B and states, "will you hook" for a potential buyer from anywhere, USA, part of the country who is looking at a light shod show horse? If the horse does well at the show you are judging you get ten percent of the sale price. The end result with this practice is the buyer gets a stepping pace horse and many buyers are none the wiser.

You need to be aware that it's not a perfect world. Giving a judge a polygraph test after a horse show and not releasing the results just makes for more unwanted speculation. A judge who comments, "The DQP checked the horse and found him sound to show. I just tied the class that's in front of me." is just shifting the burden off the one person who should excuse the horse. The judge has the overall responsibility to make the right decision for a bad-image horse.

Anyone can make a mistake on a weekend show but the stakes are high at a world-class show. How will history judge the Tennessee Walking Horse breed not crowning a 2006 World's Grand Champion? Only time will tell. It can go one of two ways. Show management's point of view was to stop the show for safety reasons, thus not letting the remaining horses that had passed the DQP inspection show to crown a world's grand champion. John Q. Public's point of view is a certain horse was supposed to win but did not check sound so the show was canceled. What does this have to do with judges? Only time will tell. Perception versus reality is alive and well in the show world.

Years ago I saw a Pony Club Rally call a vet for one horse that was presumed unsound (sore) because he was shaking his head. The vet politely told the group the horse was a gaited horse and was just fine. The perception was that the horse was sore. The reality or truth of the matter was the horse was doing a great gait. I'm not saying soring of show horses has been cleaned up, but in all fairness it has come a long way. I believe a good judge knowing his or her trade can resolve the soring matter very quickly. How the scar rule and swab testing play out will be the determining factor for the Tennessee Walking Horse show industry.

One area I find interesting in training the show horse in Kentucky I started out years ago in the Tennessee Walking Horse world with the plantation classes. The plantation horse's front ends got so big I went to the light-shod divisions. It wasn't long before the front ends with these horses got so big I went to the country pleasure divisions. Now I was lucky here. I stayed about ten years with nice, free, easy gaited horses with good sound competition. Now this division has changed into the old plantation division with a sporty lick one week and a traditional walking gait the next. It's kind of like rolling the dice. You never know what a judge will do in this division. One positive note, Kentucky has the only World's Grand Champion class available for Country Pleasure Competition.

On the good side there are good judges who take the job very seriously and do a good job of judging a horse show. When a judge does a good job there is very little uproar after the show. Not everyone is going to agree on the best horse unless it is obvious to everyone. Most certainly you can get the top three horses right in a class and personal taste goes then for number one.

You can have fun at a horse show by realizing your horse comes first and foremost, not a judge's opinion. It's been my experience that come Monday after the show the only people who remember the classes are the winners and they soon forget in the zeal of getting ready for the next show. I once had a lady tell me my horses were a trail horses. Now keep in mind they can walk with any light shod horse in America but in her eyes they were just trail horses. Kind of hurt my feelings. After winning the light shod class and observing her flying stepping pace hollow-backed horse, I knew then, we need more trail horses in the show world. Finding the right horse and developing him into a show horse is the process of fun and years of enjoyment within the show world. It's the journey with your horses that gives you the sportier lick.

Now don't discount the trail horse training methods for producing a world-class show horse. Amateur riders are proving this method every day with great success. Don't let anyone tell you the trail horses cannot be trained to same high standards we see in the show ring today. Most mainstream trail riders who are the backbone of the four industries mentioned in this book are training to a high standard with a sound horse. If you want to find a good show horse gait find a good professional endurance rider and take a good look at the show gait. I highly recommend you find the right class to show your horse. If he is a trail horse, show in trail classes. If he has some bloom and animation, lean more towards light shod classes. Bottom line is, take the family and have fun.

Chapter Twentynine: Mr. T's Prince

"When at some stage we want to become riders. Unbridled spirit forever."
G. L. Lane

At the end of this book I think of my own horse, *Mr. T's Prince*, who has given so freely of his life to make such meaning to his owner's life. He patiently helped me train countless colts over the years with his smooth flowing gait that unwaveringly taught the seat, legs, and hands.

Mr. T's Prince
(Babe's Gemini One x
Bugger's Blue Lady)

I purchased *Mr. T's Prince* when he was on his way to the stockyard. You know what that meant. He had picked up the nasty habit of kicking barn walls down. I went to look at him for a friend of mine who wanted a pleasure horse. It didn't take long to realize, when it took three people to hold him just to mount, that he was not in a pleasure horse mood. When you rode him, he would scrape your leg against the wall. Not just on one side, but both directions of travel in the barn you would get a good raking. When I could keep my legs off the wall I could feel a very powerful gait that at times was breath taking. The price was too steep for the amount of rehabilitation that was required to reclaim this horse. If he could be reprogrammed it would take a lot of time so I passed on the sale.

A week later, around midnight, I received a call from the owner who was upset with *Mr. T's Prince* for kicking the front of the stall wall down. The owner told me if I wanted the horse he would take $1,200.00, bottom price, or take pleasure in sending him to the stockyard. That was still too steep for a reclaim horse. I told him I would think about the deal and get back with him later. I still did not want the challenge, but the more I thought about this horse going to the stockyard, the more I leaned towards giving him a second chance. I stayed up all night debating with myself whether or not to buy him. The bottom line for me was if he was worth staying up all night worrying about, he was worth buying.

I started *Mr. T's Prince's* re-training on the ground just as outlined in this book. I noticed he was extremely quick about any lesson I wanted to teach. He was very athletic in his movement and especially light on the forehand. Once he understood the lesson he excelled quickly to the next lesson.

I rode a lot of times with just a rope halter so as not to hurt his mouth or cause an overreaction with the bit. I used a snaffle bit when teaching him the calm-down cue and reaching down and forward.

I gave him two options about mounting, either stand still or go to work. He figured the lesson out with some sweat time under the girth. You could see and appreciate with daily training pain, fear, excitability, and muscle tone problems disappearing with only an occasional flash back.

When he relaxed in his mind and body the turning point came with a big natural gait reserved for kings. His first show out of 26 head of horses he won the class. He went on to set the standards for lite-shod and country pleasure classes for years in Kentucky and adjoining states. I lost track of the number of blue ribbon championships at 181 blues. The Kentucky Celebration is the only World Grand Championship Country Pleasure Class offered in America. He won the 1998 Kentucky Celebration, Reserve 1999 Kentucky Celebration, Ladies Open Reserve class 2005, and Men fifty and over 2005 world championships. I would like to take credit for his accomplishment but let me assure you he achieved the standards of excellence on his own terms by being a super athlete. I played only a minor role of staying out of his way. Now it's one thing to win horse shows, but to set a standard for the entire country pleasure division is a World Class Super Horse.

Mr. T's Prince had natural ability to drive his hindquarters under his body with no wasted hock motion. In the show ring he presented a picture of, "look at me!" with the style of a champion, with ears always perked forward. When I call on him he always stays in rhythm with a great head shake and counterbalance of motion. He reaches from his shoulders and sets his front foot down as an extension of the shoulders. When he goes to pass other horses he becomes more competitive, with more head nod. He works on the bit and accepts contact naturally into a self-carriage gait.

In the wintertime, barefooted, he would not change or alter his gaits. He moved like he had a sense of purpose in life, a great desire to go forward in rhythm, timing, and balance.

In having this type of horse I wanted to learn as much as I could about what made him great without years of professional training. I broke down each area of his movement to help me understand what I was looking for in trying to teach and develop other colts to move with excellence of standards. Over the years now I have had several colts as good as *Mr. T's Prince*, but only because of his teaching ability.

After starting many colts and re-training many horses I find the classical approach is best suited for training gaited horses. A good gaited horse will make anybody look good. I have had several good offers to sell *Mr. T's Prince* but I might as well own a good horse for he is a happy student horse. I can say without reservation, many people have the privilege to view but only a few have had the honor to ride. "I hope you always ride a good horse." *Gary L. Lane*

From the Trail to the Rail